Wood Engineering
in the 21st Century:

Research Needs and Goals

**Proceedings of the Workshop
offered in conjunction with the
SEI/ASCE Structures Congress XV**

**Portland, Oregon
April 16, 1997**

**Edited by
Kenneth J. Fridley
Washington State University**

Published by

 **ASCE** American Society
of Civil Engineers

SEI

1801 Alexander Bell Drive
Reston, VA 20191-4400

Abstract: These proceedings, *Wood Engineering in the 21st Century: Research Needs and Goals,* are the product of a workshop held in conjunction with the Structural Engineering Institute (SEI) Structures Congress XV, April 16, 1997, and organized by the Technical Activities Division Committee on Wood. The primary objective of the workshop was to develop a framework for future coordinated research in wood engineering. A set of 10 position papers is included herein, along with a set of three broad-based research initiatives. Three initiatives were derived from working group discussions of research needs and prioritization. Additionally, three general needs, although not research needs, are included as they were considered to be of importance to wood engineering's future.

Library of Congress Cataloging-in-Publication Data

Wood engineering in the 21st century: research needs and goals: proceedings of the workshop offered in conjunction with the SEI/ASCE Structures Congress XV, Portland, Oregon, 16 April 1997 / edited by Kenneth J. Fridley.
p.   cm.
Includes bibliographical references and index.
ISBN 0-7844-0295-7
1. Building, Wooden–Congresses. 2. Wood–Congresses. I. Fridley, Kenneth J., 1963- .
II. American Society of Civil Engineers. III. Structures Congress (15th: 1997: Portland, Or.)
TA666.W633 1997   97-31342
624.1'84--dc21   CIP

WOOD ENGINEERING IN THE 21ST CENTURY: RESEARCH NEEDS AND GOALS

STEERING COMMITTEE:

Dr. Kenneth J. Fridley (Chair)
Washington State University

Dr. J. David Barrett
The University of British Columbia

Mr. Kenneth E. Bland, P.E.
American Forest and Paper Association

Dr. Kevin C.K. Cheung, P.E.
Western Wood Products Association

Ms. Kelley Cobeen, P.E.
GFDS Engineers / Structural Engineers Association of California

Dr. Al DeBonis
Wood Advisory Services, Inc.

Mr. David C. Fischetti, P.E.
DCF Engineers

Dr. Robert Leicester
CSIRO, Division of Building, Construction and Engineering, AUSTRALIA

Dr. Hideo Sugiyama
Science University of Tokyo, JAPAN

Dr. Lawrence A. Soltis, P.E.
U.S. Forest Products Laboratory

WOOD ENGINEERING IN THE 21ST CENTURY:
RESEARCH NEEDS AND GOALS

SPONSORED BY:

American Society of Civil Engineers

Wood Products Promotion Council:

American Forest & Paper Association
APA – The Engineered Wood Association
Canadian Wood Council
Southern Forest Products Association
Western Wood Products Association
Florida Wood Council

US Forest Products Laboratory

International Staple, Nail and Tool Association (ISANTA)

Washington State University
Department of Civil and Environmental Engineering
Wood Materials and Engineering Laboratory

Virginia Tech, Department of Wood Science and Forest Products

National Science Foundation

USDA, National Research Initiative, Competitive Grants Program

CO-SPONSORED BY:

Weyerhaeuser

Oregon State University, Department of Forest Products

Purdue University, Wood Research Laboratory

Southern Pine Inspection Bureau

OTHER SPONSORS:

Engineering Data Management

Forest Products Society

Society of Wood Science and Technology

ACKNOWLEDGEMENTS

A workshop such as **Wood Engineering in the 21st Century: Research Needs and Goals** could not be successfully undertaken without significant financial support and volunteer effort. The former came from various industrial, academic, and governmental sources as listed previously. Without the financial support from these sources, this workshop would never have been possible. The volunteer effort can be initially defined by the steering committee listed under separate heading. I wish to single out, however, Dr. Kevin C.K. Cheung, Western Wood Products Association, who, in addition to serving on the Workshop Steering Committee, was our contact with the SEI Structures Congress Steering Committee and served as chair of the Technical Activities Division Committee on Wood. Dr. Cheung was a valuable point of contact throughout the process. In addition to the steering committee, I wish to thank all the position paper authors who graciously shared their knowledge and expertise with the workshop participants. Additionally, Dr. Marvin Criswell, Colorado State University, who summarized all the position papers into a single presentation with an amazing level of completeness, has my sincere thanks and respect. A genuine expression of gratitude also goes to the workshop group facilitators who, in addition to taking on the difficult task of coordinating the effort of their groups during the working sessions, had to communicate the thoughts and ideas of their groups. Taking preliminary reports from the group facilitators and providing a preview of outcomes to participants were Dr. Vijaya Gopu, Louisiana State University, and Ms. Catherine Marx, Southern Forest Products Association, both of whom did an outstanding job that was appreciated by all participants. Assisting the facilitators, participants, and Dr. Gopu and Ms. Marx throughout the workshop were four students from Washington State University: Mr. Steven Davidow, Ms. Kristine Fromhold, Mr. Brian Tucker, and Mr. Judsen Williams. Many of the facilitators, in addition to their work during the workshop, served as writers and reviewers for the final set of research needs. Taking a lead role in the editing of the research need statements was Dr. Donald Bender, Washington State University, whose editing skills and technical vision were a benefit to the workshop. I wish also to acknowledge and thank Dr. Ronald Sack, National Science Foundation, for providing a thought-provoking keynote address. Finally, I wish to thank Ms. Jane Finch-Howell, Western Wood Products Association, for the cover design and art work.

Kenneth J. Fridley
Workshop Chair

PREFACE

These proceedings are the product of a workshop entitled **Wood Engineering in the 21st Century: Research Needs and Goals**. The primary objective of the workshop was to develop a framework for future, coordinated research in wood engineering. This requires defining the state-of-the-art of wood engineering, developing goals for the 21st century, establishing a set of research initiatives, and disseminating the information. For the purposes of this workshop, wood engineering is defined to range from fundamental material properties to heavy timber construction. To fulfill the stated objective, input from a wide range of interests was necessary. Therefore, the workshop included participation from all sectors of the wood engineering community, including design professionals, code-writing agencies, wood industry organizations, government and university researchers, etc. This is evidenced by simply examining the list of nearly 100 participants at the end of these proceedings.

To provide the necessary background for workshop participants, invited authors prepared, in parallel, position papers which were made available to the workshop attendees. The topics and authors of these position papers were established by the steering committee.

Working groups were organized at the Workshop to establish specific research priorities. Participants were assigned to a working group such that each working group had a balance of researchers, practitioners and industry representatives. Volunteer "facilitators" were trained to lead working group discussions. The facilitators also provided a report of their group's work to the steering committee. A committee comprised of selected facilitators then compiled these reports into a set of research initiatives. Three broad-based research initiatives, with each initiative having specific action items required to achieve the objective of the initiative, were the end result of this process. Additionally, three other areas of need were defined and are included in these proceedings, but these were not deemed "research" in the strictest sense.

All papers with defined authorship included in these proceedings were selected and reviewed by members of the workshop steering committee. All other papers were the result of the committee process as outlined above. All papers are eligible for discussion in the Journal of Structural Engineering. The papers are also eligible for ASCE awards.

This workshop, like its predecessor in 1983, was successful in that it provided a forum for the free exchange of ideas and needs by practicing engineers, industry leaders, and researchers. The challenges facing wood engineering research are now defined and it is our collective responsibility to see that we advance the state-of-the-art accordingly.

CONTENTS

BENEFITS FROM WOOD ENGINEERING RESEARCH

Susan L. LeVan[1]

Forests play a critical role in the environmental and economic health of the world. The world population continues to grow with an associated increase in demand for paper and wood products. Increasingly, forests are being recognized as more than simple photosynthesis factories. Forests are recognized as the "environmental capital" that provides the basis for a wide spectrum of benefits. Forest ecosystems provide watershed protection, nutrient cycling, a moderating influence on global climate, and serve as a repository for biological and genetic diversity. Many of these uses and benefits are complimentary. However, some are not and this leads to increased competition and conflicts, especially between meeting the nation's need for wood and fiber versus meeting society's expectation for a healthy environment. Throughout the 1970s and 1980s, the competing uses of U.S. forests have been the source of a persistent and often acrimonious debate. That same debate took place on a global scale at the United Nations Conference on environment and Development (UNCED) in 1992. Follow-up discussions have lead to formal recognition of sustainability as the over arching issue facing the world and the fact that environmental and economic issues cannot be easily separated.

In the future, this same acrimonious debate is anticipated to move beyond the stage of debate and into the realm of public policy. Thus, as we develop research needs in wood engineering, we know that three primary issues will affect the use of wood as a building material. These three primary issues are (1) increasing the demand for all uses of forests, (2) changing the forest resource base, and (3) increasing environmental concerns that production and use of wood are causing deterioration of the environment.

Increased Demand

In the United States, the wood and fiber portion of the forest products sector is a significant component of economic activity, employing approximately 1.4 million people. In 1994, primary forest products were valued at more than $19

---

[1] Assistant Director, Wood Products Research, US Forest Products Laboratory, Madison, WI.

billion, and secondary forest products at nearly $75 billion. This represents about 2% of the Gross Domestic Product (GDP) for goods and services and about 1% of the total GDP. Thus, forest products provide a significant contribution to the economic vitality of the United States.

The demand for fiber and wood products has not abated. The total world economy is growing faster than population growth. The World Bank estimates that within the next 30 years, average per capita income worldwide could reach the same level as the top 20% of the countries of the world. Jaakko Poyry forecasts that consumer demand for fiber in developing countries will grow as a function of increasing population, literacy rates, and the standard of living. The expanding population and world economy are also influenced by the increasing demand for housing. One-tenth of the global economy is derived from constructing homes and offices, and a significant amount of people live and work in wood-frame buildings. Globally, housing construction accounts for more than 25% of the world's demand for solid wood in products, ranging from lumber to oriented strandboard. Residential construction is the dominant market for the solid-wood sector in the United States. Although anticipated demand for U.S. housing starts is expected to be relatively stable for the next several decades, the size of houses is changing. During the last 40 years, the average size of single-family housing units has nearly doubled, offsetting any trend of declining wood used per square meter of floor area. Thus, this offsetting results in a trend toward increasing average lumber used per single family unit.

Resource Base

Forest conditions in the United States have changed over time. Today, the growth to harvest ratio for all species is 1.33, but the species and the mix have changed, material is smaller and often of lower quality. The growth to harvest ratio for softwoods is 1.09, for hardwoods 1.80. The vast, unreserved volume of softwood timber in the United States does not exist any more. Also, concern regarding the health of U.S. forests is increasing. Between 1986 and 1991, timber mortality increased almost 25%. Many second-growth stands in the West, where fire has been excluded for many decades, now contain dense, overstocked understories. Infestations by insects and pests have left some stands with significant amounts of dead and dying material, causing tremendous build-up of fuel loadings. In the North and East, there are significant quantities of mature hardwoods. In addition, these forests have been high-graded over the centuries. Therefore, we need to remove some of these lower quality hardwoods to restore these stands to healthy ecosystems.

Thus, the primary characterization of tomorrow's forest resources is variability. We will see many different species, from a variety of sources, as our raw material. We will see the average diameter of the logs, at least for the next 50 years, remain on its decreasing trend, especially in the West. The norm will become mixed species of lower quality rather than the traditional quality used. Increasing quantities of lower quality hardwoods will be used for structural applications, primarily produced on nonmanaged, nonindustrial private lands. At the same time, we will also see an increase in the use of plantation logs, both domestic and imported, as well as increased quantities of recycled wood, which may contain contaminants. In the forests, we will see more selective harvesting, less clearcutting, increases in the numbers of snags and old-growth trees left standing, and greater attention to increasing the biodiversity of the forest.

Environmental Concerns

People want clean air, clean water, unspoiled lands, and healthy forests. However, increasing perceptions link environmental degradation with product and use of wood and fiber products. The U.S. Clean Air Act of 1992 placed great emphasis on eliminating ozone and other noxious gas components, such as volatile organic compounds (VOCs). The forest products industry is one of the largest manufacturing sectors contributing to the emission of VOC's, primarily through drying of wood and chips. The Clean Water Act of 1972 brought point sources of pollution under control. Nevertheless, non-source pollution, which can be caused from sedimentation resulting from forest roads and timber harvesting, are often identified as a key problem.

Addressing the Issues

People need products and services from forests, they want jobs, and they expect a clean environment. These needs and expectations puts us heading for a collision course. However, history has shown that technological advances have often helped mitigate such collisions. Technological advances in wood engineering are no exception. However, the technological advances in wood engineering will need to simultaneously address the following issues:

- Conserve wood and fiber resources
- Help restore healthy and resilient forest ecosystems.
- Avoid or mitigate environmental impacts

Improvements in wood utilization from the tree to the final product have demonstrated significant savings in the forest resource by reducing material losses during, harvesting and processing. Since the turn of the century, the ratio of product output to resource input has been increasing. The efficiency has increased because of technologies that have improved the proficiency of converting trees and logs into products. Today, and in the near-term future, improvements in wood utilization to conserve our forest resource will depend on technological advances in the ways that we "use" our forest resources, while helping to restore forest ecosystems and minimize environmental impacts. Recent trends in the wood-frame housing area highlight some of the improvements in how we use wood products.

Changes are also anticipated in the type of wood products that will be used for housing. Much of the increased demand in the United States will occur in the Structural and nonstructural engineered wood products markets. Oriented strandboard and waferboard are increasingly being substituted for softwood plywood. The use of other engineered wood products is also increasing dramatically.

Laminated veneer lumber has also steadily increased, with capacity at about 1 million cubic meters in 1996. The primary reason for such growth is that these products arc more flexible in using a diverse raw material base. 'I he traditional lumber market is expected to remain stable or maintain a slight growth.

Challenges

What does this mean to those of us involved in wood engineering? The challenge for wood engineers is to develop cost-effective technologies that allow the forest products industry to make wood products from a raw material that is lower in quality, contains more variability, meets late 20th century end-use performance specifications, and still turns a profit. Technological advances in wood engineering that need to be accomplished to meet this challenge (while using the diverse resource anticipated) can be classified in the following four areas: (1) engineering wood composites to meet specific end-use performance requirements; (2) improving engineering design to reduce dependence on "redundancy" as a safety factor; (3) developing ways to ensure quality and in-service performance for wood components, assemblies, and structures; and (4) increasing the durability of wood components and structures.

The consequences of "not" meeting the challenge will effect everyone. If we do not remove the excessive, low quality biomass that exists in both our public and nonindustrial private forests, then we are placing our forests at a greater risk of attack by insects, diseases, and ultimately catastrophic wildfires, particularly in the \Vest. The consequences of such wildfires include greater erosion, less capability of the soil to hold water, increased sedimentation of streams, increased runoff into watersheds, increased mortality to freshwater fish and those above fish on the foodchain, delayed regeneration of our forests, increased air pollution, and significant impact on climate changes. These are major environmental consequences that affect everyone's quality of life.

Wood engineering disciplines have a major technological challenge. However, the challenge to policymakers and others who provide financial support is greater. There are two ways to mitigate the threats to our forests:

- Money could be allocated to remove the sign)e buildup of excessive biomass, with treatment costs ranging from, about $300 to 500/acre. With approximately 39 million acres of public lands that need such treatment, revenues needed are $15 billion.

- Uses for this excessive biomass will help offset some of the costs.

This document highlights the technical challenges that lay ahead for wood engineers. As you read this document, it clearly shows that the challenges are indeed significant. However, I believe that the wood engineering community has the technology and skills to accomplish the task. Of greater concern are the financial and policy decisions by those who will provide funding to support the outlined research needs. The question now becomes, "How can we afford the consequences of not funding such research efforts?"

CRITICAL RESEARCH NEED: BEHAVIOR AND PERFORMANCE OF NEW AND EXISTING WOOD STRUCTURES

SCOPE AND DEFINITION:

Engineering research on wood "structures" in the past 25 years has largely focused on the performance of individual members, connections, and discrete subassemblies such as shear walls, floors, roof trusses, and diaphragms. This has been appropriate given the limited public funding available and the need to develop a basic understanding of these elements. It has also been critical in spurring industry to develop new products and materials. However, the performance of the entire structural system is of greatest long-term interest to consumers and society. Whether the issue is serviceability, extended life, or natural hazard damage mitigation, acceptable performance of the entire building system is a key goal in meeting our national need for affordable, durable, functional, and long-lasting housing and commercial structures.

Achieving that goal requires an understanding of how complex wood structural systems respond to a myriad of imperfectly known loads and other service-related actions. This research initiative addresses that need and has two principal components: (1) Systems behavior and performance of new and existing wood structures, and (2) extending the service life and functionality of wood structures.

Systems behavior and performance of new and existing wood structures

Residential and commercial structures respond to loads such as occupancy, wind, or snow as a system of structural elements. It is the right combination and placement of elements with appropriate size and material that gives the structure its integrity and serviceability. With most structures, including those of steel, concrete, or wood, we can make reasonable engineering judgments about expected loadings and how forces are distributed throughout a structural system. Engineering principles then enable component or subassembly design. Some systems judgments are based on engineering principles, others on experience or rational assumptions. When systems or loadings become complex, then our assumptions may become more conservative to account for ignorance, or they can be simply wrong. Furthermore, the true balance between safety and economy often is unknown.

One example is with simple wood-frame house construction, which is generally not engineered and may be covered by conventional construction standards based on history rather than engineering analysis. The North American tradition of light-frame systems has a long record of satisfactory performance, although not without some blemishes. If materials, housing styles, site characteristics, labor costs, craftsman skills, societal expectations, and a myriad of other factors remained static, then the need for engineering these structures could be moot. They are not static, however, when we use traditional engineering analyses using tributary area methods for expected loads we discover that some materials and components may not possess the requisite strength or stiffness. Since we know many of these materials and components have provided decades of economic and satisfactory performance, then we must begin to suspect some part of the design process. Recent research in floor and roof systems has shown that tributary area analysis is in error for sheathed framing members and that applied load is actually shared by several members. This kind of systems analysis, directed at subassemblies is beginning to tell us ways to improve our designs. This suggests that the performance, economy, or safety of an entire structural system (e.g., a house) can be improved by understanding how subassemblies and inter-component connections function together in resisting service and extreme-event loads.

Extending the service life and functionality of wood structures

If the effective service life of wood structures could be extended, then many long-term benefits would accrue to both society and consumers. This is true for both existing structures and those yet to be built. This research initiative focuses on the need for an integrated approach to design, construction, maintenance, and renovation that precludes premature failure or loss of functionality and allows for more long-term efficiency and life. It also addresses the need for repair of damaged structures and renovation of those whose serviceability or economic value has been impaired.

Although wood structures are comprised of many wood and non-wood elements, with both non-structural and structural functions, the economic and practical value of the structure depends on the performance of the structural skeleton and all attachments as a system. The foundation or structural frame is often the key to adjust the usefulness or function of the whole system. For example, in the aftermath of Hurricane Andrew, investigators discovered that key sections of the gable ends of houses failed under high wind. This resulted in localized or catastrophic roof failure that exposed the interior contents to rain, causing high financial losses. Another example might be a new use of an existing structure that causes excessive vibration or deflection, thus limiting its use. Loss of functionality can be a burden equal to or greater than that of structural failure.

Often, an inability to make a rational assessment of the safety and serviceability of a structural system precludes extending service life. Cost-effective, nondestructive means of evaluating strength and stiffness of members, connections, and systems are needed to make accurate assessments of residual strength of damaged structures or for potential safety upgrading of undamaged structures. New, innovative repair and renovation techniques will also need to be developed and verified once accurate assessments are made.

IMPACT/IMPLICATIONS

Success with this research initiative will directly lead to more cost effective and safe wood structures in the United States. Since the majority of wood structures are residential, the general public will benefit from safer and more affordable housing. Timber structures are also a significant and growing portion of the commercial and transportation structures in the United States. This research will enable expansion of cost-effective commercial wood structures that support small to medium-size business and that in rural areas. Ultimately, society will also benefit by an increased pool of structures that can be economically repaired and rehabilitated to meet the changing needs of the 21st century. Collateral benefits will also accrue to society and industry through the opportunity to utilize renewable wood-based resources more efficiently and to integrate more innovative value-added products into structures.

RECOMMENDED ACTIONS

Within the scope of this research initiative, the following areas of research are needed:

- Develop an understanding of the behavior and performance of structures, including load-sharing and other system effects in structures of widely varying geometry. This understanding of basic behavior and performance needs to be translated into design and performance criteria that can be easily integrated into the design process.

- Develop performance and assessment criteria for structural system serviceability criteria, including vibration, drift, and creep.

- Develop hybrid structural systems or subassemblies that capitalize on the economy and flexibility of wood and the unique characteristics of other materials to create economy and efficiency in the final product.

- Develop technology to evaluate and monitor the performance of structures over time and during short-term extreme load events using economic and accurate nondestructive and non-intrusive methods. This performance information needs to be systematically integrated into efforts to improve codes and professional practices.

- Develop and promote new means to prevent deterioration of new and existing structures that are low cost, reliable, easily inspected/evaluated, and easily implemented.

- Develop technology and standard methods to assess residual strength and performance of damaged structural systems. Develop repair practices and methods that result in verifiable performance.

CRITICAL RESEARCH NEED: INTEGRATED ANALYSIS, DESIGN, AND CONTRUCTION METHODOLOGIES FOR WOOD STRUCTURES

SCOPE AND DEFINITION

Integrated analysis, design, and construction methodologies are needed to improve the ability of the engineer to provide safe, economical, and durable wood structures. These improvements will reduce misinterpretations between all parties and help ensure proper construction and inspection practices. Through an integrated engineering cycle, defined herein to be the continuum of engineering throughout the design/build process, the changing nature of wood materials, advances in our understanding of member and system performance, and feedback from end-users of the structures are all included. The fundamental assumption underlying this integrated approach is that without completing the described complete and integrated cycle, a constructed facility (or any other system) cannot be considered to be 'engineered.' The traditional paradigm implied in building design is: analysis leading to design and subsequent construction. However, in the case of wood construction, this has often simply been: construction. A representation of the integrated engineering analysis, design, and construction cycle with used feedback is illustrated in Fig. 1.

Wood systems, including wood materials, structural members, and connections, pose unique problems for structural analysis and predictions of both short and long-term behavior. Furthermore, relatively little attention has been paid to the engineering performance of typical light-frame construction. In order to firmly place wood design, including hybrid (e.g., wood and steel) design using wood and wood-based materials, on a sound and competitive engineering basis, the underlying assumptions used for analysis and design must be validated. With the move to place wood on the same engineered design basis as competing structural materials, there is a need to quantify (assure) the engineering performance of wood and wood-based materials in structural applications.

Integrated design tools will allow owners and architects to visualize structures from a three-dimensional perspective and "walk through" the structure in a virtual sense to obtain as realistic understanding of the final form. This will allow the function of structures to be monitored prior to construction. The tools should

9

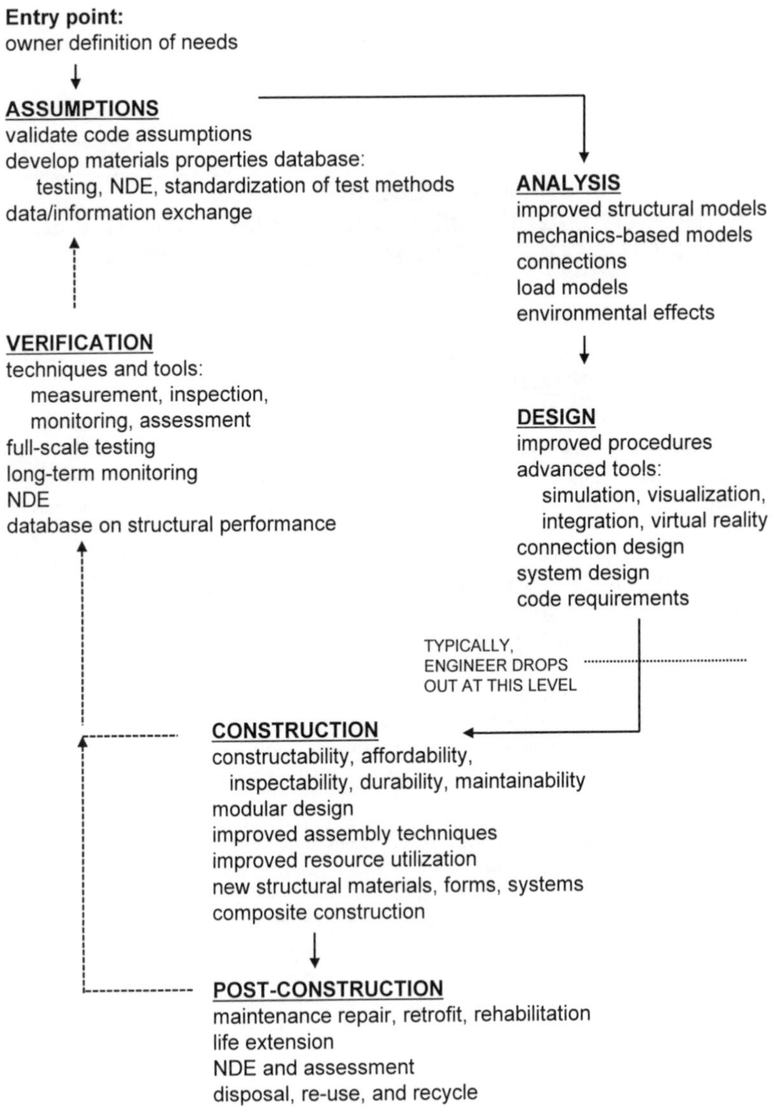

Entry point:
owner definition of needs

↓

ASSUMPTIONS
validate code assumptions
develop materials properties database:
    testing, NDE, standardization of test methods
data/information exchange

ANALYSIS
improved structural models
mechanics-based models
connections
load models
environmental effects

↓

VERIFICATION
techniques and tools:
    measurement, inspection,
    monitoring, assessment
full-scale testing
long-term monitoring
NDE
database on structural performance

DESIGN
improved procedures
advanced tools:
    simulation, visualization,
    integration, virtual reality
connection design
system design
code requirements

TYPICALLY,
ENGINEER DROPS
OUT AT THIS LEVEL

CONSTRUCTION
constructability, affordability,
    inspectability, durability, maintainability
modular design
improved assembly techniques
improved resource utilization
new structural materials, forms, systems
composite construction

↓

POST-CONSTRUCTION
maintenance repair, retrofit, rehabilitation
life extension
NDE and assessment
disposal, re-use, and recycle

FIG. 1: Integrated Analysis, Design and Construction Cycle.

then provide information to architects and engineers where design calculations are required and where architectural details may cause serviceability problems such as decay or vibration. Integrated tools should provide a bill of materials to assist in more uniform bid parameters, and eliminate the potential for special connection hardware being overlooked. Finally, integrated tools should provide information to the contractor on locations that require special attention during construction. These locations should also be communicated to building inspectors, along with any additional inspection requirements, to ensure proper oversight. If implemented properly, such advanced design tools would reduce or eliminate the misuse of different materials in structures, increase the probability that structures will perform as intended, and improve the serviceability, reliability, and longevity of wood structures.

Design tools should allow designers to design complete structures as three-dimensional systems with the ability to account for load sharing, and load and displacement redistribution. Current design methods assume structures are collages of individual components that act independently to resist loads applied or experienced. Advanced, integrated design tools should allow structures to be analyzed and designed to take advantage of the interaction of components, and actively arrange and size members, components, and sub-assemblies to share the loads and deflections. Special inter-element connection criteria will have to be established depending on the life-safety and serviceability criteria used for design, and these criteria need to be included in the design tools. Accounting for system performance of structures will reduce the volume of materials required and improve the serviceability and reliability of the final product.

Another essential criterion for advanced design and analysis tools is the integration of non-structural systems and elements into the structural system. For instance, a building system design should include locations of mechanical, electrical, and plumbing systems that ensure the structural system is not adversely effected by non-structural systems. Typically, contractors modify the structural system to install heating, plumbing, and electrical systems. This results in two problems. First, the structural system must be over-designed to account for the unknown modifications that will be made to install the non-structural systems while maintaining the safety and serviceability of the building. Second, the structural system is often compromised by the modifications, resulting in safety or performance problems that must be repaired, after the fact.

IMPACT/IMPLICATIONS

The impact and implications of developing integrated analysis, design, and construction methodolgies have tremendous effects on the engineered wood structures. Engineers and architects will be able to improve performance while reducing wasted material by integrating the non-structural systems and components into the structural system, and buildings will have improved serviceability and longevity due to information indicating locations of potential problems such as decay or vibration. Construction safety, costs, and duration will also be improved by new technologies being developed to address system performance in design. New structural systems that incorporate many of the non-structural systems and components will spawn new tools, materials, and methods of construction that will reduce the cost and time of construction, while improving on-site safety.

In order for wood construction to compete on the same economic, safety, and performance bases as competitive materials, not to mention at a level demanded by the general public and end-users, steps must be taken to validate its potential as an engineered system. This is not a small task. Most wood construction has long been thought of as non-engineered and more of a trade than a science. In general, wood structures have performed well over time, even when subject to extreme events such as earthquakes and hurricanes. However, losses due to these and other natural hazards have increased pressures on builders and owners to minimize construction and materials costs. Further, competing materials such as cold-formed steel have made significant in-roads into the market with cost-competitive alternatives to traditional light-frame (wood) construction. Only recently (i.e., in the past decade) has significant attention been paid to evaluating the engineering performance of wood structural systems in the built environment. This has posed a number of challenges including how to account for time effects (load duration, creep), environmental effects (moisture, temperature, exposure), and system effects (load-sharing, load-distribution, element interaction). In addition, there have been significant challenges posed by the variety of construction techniques and materials used, the range of connection types and associated hardware, and the issue of durability and long-term structural performance/integrity.

RECOMMENDED ACTIONS

Development of integrated analysis, design, and construction methodologies requires an understanding of the system performance of structures, the function of non-structural systems and components, and the construction process. Research is needed in the following areas:

- Develop performance criteria and integrated analysis/design tools for whole structures, including simplified, rational design procedures that account for load sharing and other system effects in structures of widely varying geometry.

- Develop assessment methods and design standards for structural system serviceability criteria including vibration, drift, and creep.

- Develop and encourage a multi-disciplinary approach to structural design, construction maintenance and renovation that incorporates broad professional expertise. This would include architects, lenders, engineers, manufacturers, fabricators, contractors, and owners.

- Develop design criteria and methodologies for rehabilitation and retrofit of existing building inventory, including methods for including information from non-destructive evaluations (NDE) and assessments of wood members and structures.

- Assess environmental effects, including durability, on wood and wood-based materials and include appropriate design criteria for such factors in the design process.

CRITICAL RESEARCH NEED: DEVELOPMENT OF WOOD-BASED COMPOSITE MATERIALS

SCOPE AND DEFINITION

As a structural material, wood is unique because it is renewable. Historically, this fact has fostered its use through widespread availability, familiarity, and a good cost-performance ratio. However, available timber resources are declining in both quality and quantity. A critical need exists to extend and sustain the changing wood resource through development of advanced wood-based materials and functional elements.

In the past, wood-based composite materials were composed mostly of wood fiber with only small amounts of polymeric adhesives. These materials were designed to look and behave like solid wood with improvements in variability, element geometry, or cost. With the advent of engineered wood products, a new class of performance-driven materials has grown. Although these materials have originally been focused on structural applications, growth opportunities are also present in non-structural applications where moisture and decay resistance may be more important than increased strength and stiffness.

Here, wood-based materials are defined as any substance that is at least 50% wood by weight and is useful in manufacturing some functional element. This includes, but is not restricted to solid wood, traditional wood composites (i.e., plywood, OSB, particleboard, etc.), composites of wood and synthetics (i.e., wood-plastic composites, inorganic-bonded wood composites, etc.), and composites with integral fiber reinforcement.

In contrast, a functional element is some assemblage produced in whole or part from a wood-based material. This can be an assembly of different wood-based materials (i.e., I-joists, trusses, etc.) or combinations of wood with synthetic materials (i.e., FRP reinforced glulam, structural insulated panels, etc.). Finally, a structural system is comprised of a related series of functional elements.

The objective of the aforementioned definitions is to draw a distinction between the design associated with materials and that needed for functional elements and systems. All levels are relevant and valuable for extending and improving the

15

utilization of wood resources, however, they must be considered as distinct to be fully exploited. In addition, the concept of design must be extended past the pure calculation of loads and deflections typically used in structures.

IMPACT/IMPLICATIONS

In recent years, a revolution has begun in the area of wood structures. This change has evolved through the continued and steady introduction of different engineered wood components in building construction. The engineering community has generally welcomed this move to more reliable and highly engineered wood-based materials. However, there is concern that these new materials be thoroughly characterized from a number of aspects such as biodegradation, moisture resistance, creep, and fatigue. Recent trends towards wood composites and functional elements that combine wood and synthetic materials to enhance specific performance criteria have positive implications. The largest potential gain lies in extending the performance envelope of wood into aggressive environments and demanding load applications. This will support a move toward further combinations of wood with other building materials in structural systems. Aggressive pursuit of this track will not only thwart the continued erosion of traditional wood applications to synthetics, but potentially expand uses into those traditionally dominated by steel and concrete. In addition, a widespread evaluation of these hybrid composites with traditional wood materials and synthetics will likely bolster the confidence in wood construction in general.

RECOMMENDED ACTIONS

The following are recommendations for development of advanced wood-based materials that efficiently utilize our changing wood resource:

- Develop a comprehensive understanding of fundamental properties of materials used in wood-based composites.

- Understand how changes in the wood resource will influence the performance and economic future of wood materials.

- Aggressively support the development and understanding of hybrid wood composites, functional wood elements, and structural systems.

- Thoroughly evaluate the performance of wood-based materials and functional elements with synthetic counterparts to understand, improve, and exploit their strengths.

- Improve the durability of wood-based materials. Durability evaluations should address long-term performance, including biodegradation, moisture resistance, dimensional stability, creep, creep-rupture, and fatigue.

- Produce accelerated test methodologies for assessing the durability of wood-based materials. These methodologies should accurately represent field conditions and response, be based in engineering theory, and be easily adapted to structural design.

OTHER NEEDS IN WOOD ENGINEERING

During the workshop, several groups separately identified three areas of need that, although not "research" in the strictest sense, are still worthy of inclusion here as they are strongly linked to the previously outlined critical research needs. That is, within each of the critical research need areas, the following points of general need should be considered and addressed wherever possible.

WOOD ENGINEERING EDUCATION

Wood is one of the earliest known building materials, yet even today, it is often misused in structures. A significant reason is the limited education of producers and users of wood. Therefore, wood engineering education is a critical need.

Scope and Definition

There is a crisis in wood engineering education on a worldwide basis. This crisis has led and continues to lead to misuse and under utilization of wood in structural applications. Wood will continue to be an important construction material throughout the world. Its efficient use will ensure a sustainable supply. Education is key to improving effective and efficient utilization of wood in structural applications.

Wood engineering education is needed at all levels of use and production including, but not limited to: secondary schools; technical and vocational schools (community colleges); universities (e.g., undergraduate and graduate level in Civil Engineering, Forest Products, Agricultural Engineering, Architecture, Construction Engineering/Management, Material Science); practicing engineers, architects and other professionals associated with specifying and designing wood products for structural applications; building inspectors/code officials; and other users (all people involved in wood construction, e.g., fabricators, framers, builders). Wood engineering education encompasses everything from basic wood (including all wood-based composites) properties/behavior to designing simple and complex wood and hybrid (wood in combination with other materials) structures (including connections, components, etc.). It should also include thorough coverage of wood technology including durability issues, grading, and life-cycle analysis of various wood-based materials and components.

Impact/Implications

A well-coordinated effort is required by all facets of the wood industry and academic communities to educate future wood engineers for the 21st century. To achieve effective and efficient wood engineering education in the United States, the wood industry must take an active role and be available to provide assistance to educational institutions.

Recommended Actions

To address the need for increased wood engineering education, academia and industry must work together on several fronts. First, curricula must be developed for different departments to meet the educational needs of different students at universities. Second, course must be developed and offered for practicing engineers/architects (continuing education). Guidelines (or manuals) need to be made available for on-site inspection of wood buildings and supervision of wood construction. Discussion should be initiated between industry members and university professors to provide an opportunity to exchange information. Finally, the Internet and World Wide Web need to be fully utilized to facilitate the exchange of information about latest/current technology/products.

STANDARDS AND CODES HARMONIZATION

Standards and codes harmonization is needed to facilitate materials and systems development, effective market implementation, and is a critical need with respect to the implementation of new building and material technologies resulting from directed research efforts such as those described previously.

Scope and Definition

Examples of testing and material standards include but are not limited to those promulgated by the American Society for Testing and Materials (ASTM), International Standards Organization (ISO), European Committee for Standardization (CEN), Canadian Standards Association (CSA), and many product-based associations. In the United States, ASTM standards are typically used to direct tests and product development. However, when products or other regulations are intended for international markets, differing standards can become trade barriers.

Examples of incompatibility between test or product standards exist for methods of evaluating connections, assemblies, and material properties. If prior consideration were given when conceptualizing and writing standards, incompatibilities could be minimized. If harmonization is not accomplished, then these incompatibilities may be used as tools to restrict trade and the progress of technology. A crucial element to harmonization is that methods and practices of evaluation should be consistent across materials. That is, methods of assessing structural behavior or performance should share a common philosophical, if not procedural methodology, for steel, wood, concrete and other materials used in structural applications. As an example, the dynamic performance of a light frame structure should be evaluated by the same method regardless of whether the frame is made from light-gauge steel, sawn lumber products, or structural insulated panels. Research is needed to develop satisfactory test methods so performance can be directly compared for alternative material systems.

International harmonization of material standards is important to the global economy, but even within the United States, harmonization of the building codes is important. Currently, three model building codes are used in the United States, and in addition, several states and local jurisdictions promulgate their own. This collection of building codes requires that planners, designers, and builders working in multiple jurisdictions maintain multiple building codes for reference. The matter is further complicated when the jurisdictions change their reference model building code. Each time a building code revision is issued, the model code references, such as the *National Design Specification for Wood Construction*® *(NDS*®*)*, are updated in an effort to maintain the current state of design technology. Without a common building code, planners and designers may inadvertently design with the wrong edition of the design specification. Furthermore, if a particular jurisdiction does not adopt the most recent edition of the building code, designers may not be able to obtain copies of the required but outdated design specifications. These problems illustrate the need to provide a harmonized building code for the United States.

The European Community has adopted a common building code for the design and construction of buildings across all member states. In the United states, an effort is currently underway between the three model building code agencies, the Federal Emergency Management Administration (FEMA), and related industrial interests to produce the International Building Code (IBC). This building code would combine the three building codes into a single code for the United States. This effort should be supported by the timber engineering and design communities as a mechanism that will provide significant progress toward harmonization for the building regulation community in the United States.

Impact and Implications

The harmonization of codes and standards both nationally, internationally, and across materials requires concessions and consensus among all parties impacted by the regulation. Individuals or special interests parties cannot dictate the adoption of harmonized standards and codes. Harmonization also requires that the parties affected by the end product be involved in the development process. Although consensus standards are difficult to modify, the result can be enhanced by the additional scrutiny given to each proposed change.

Recommended Actions

International harmonization of standards is a difficult issue to address, because a large number of product and test standard organizations exist globally. However, if the wood products industry is to compete in a global market, harmonization of certain key standards is essential. To accomplish this, committees writing standards must invite a wide range of representation and review existing standards from other organizations prior to writing new standards. Research should be implemented that brings the philosophical and methodological evaluation of alternative materials in structural systems to commonality. This will require a multi-dimensional harmonization across materials and geographic regions.

The United States is the only industrialized country that does not have a national building code. This has hindered introduction of technology in the past and will continue to be an issue until a significant effort is made to introduce and maintain a single building code for all jurisdictions in the country. Harmonization of the model building codes is currently in progress. However, adoption of the resulting building code is not ensured, and an effort to educate and convince individual jurisdictions to adopt the code in the year 2000 will be required. In addition, jurisdictions that have not adopted a building code should be encouraged to adopt the IBC when it is ready.

ENGINEERING DATABASE FOR WOOD-BASED MATERIALS AND STRUCTURES

Development of a comprehensive engineering database on wood and wood-composite materials for researchers, designers, product manufacturers, and code officials is needed. The engineering database should include everything from basic material properties to design recommendations for engineered wood products.

Scope and Definition

In spite of flat or declining funding for research and development, technical data[1] are being generated at an explosive rate. The data sources lie in a wide variety of organizations including, but not limited to: academic institutions, government labs, professional societies, product manufacturers, codes and standards bodies, and trade associations. The types of data are just as varied as the sources. Some of the data that would be organized in the database include: solid-sawn lumber, wood/non-wood hybrid products, world-wide species properties, world-wide industry terminology, metrication data, product standards, re-used and recycled materials, and design standards & recommendations

The outlets for dissemination include technical publications, presentations at professional meetings, product literature, text and reference books, standards, and building codes. Individuals, who desire to find and use this data, and those who might not even be aware of its existence, are unnecessarily encumbered in their data search. The materials they seek might be known to them but not readily available. In other cases, they might be confident that certain data exist, but they do not know how to locate it. Ultimately, the utility of the data might be lost due to excessive time delays in acquiring access to it.

Hence, a critical need exists to develop, maintain, and publicize a world–wide database for wood and wood-composite materials and products. The most likely medium for the database is the World Wide Web (WWW) service of the global Internet.

Impact/Implications

A global database for the wood industry, representing the interests of forestry, wood science and technology, wood engineering, wood construction, and wood products has the potential to improve utilization of wood and wood products through better organization and more efficient transfer of information. Global recognition and support of the database are critical elements to its success as a central hub to the vast collection of wood engineering data available to interested parties. Development of the database has the potential to lower costs associated with generating, disseminating, and using the data. Hence, the reliability of the data will be improved and the understanding of its proper interpretation and use will be enhanced. The database will help practicing engineers, code officials, building owners and others remain current with the rapid changes in the wood industry.

---

[1] For brevity, the term *data* will be used in a general sense to include numerical values, descriptive characteristics, textual information, code provisions, recommendations for design and construction, etc.

Recommended Actions

Numerous web sites and databases already exist around the world. These initial efforts at developing a global wood database each makes an important and unique contribution toward the overall objective. However, no single effort is likely to achieve its ultimate objective. The following issues must be addressed prior to any formal movement toward a global database for wood:

Central Administration. For a global database to be globally accepted as authoritative and reliable, a cooperative administrative structure must be established to set guidelines under which the database is to be developed and maintained, including the implementation of an appropriate security system.

Funding. Once the administrative control is established, development and maintenance of the database will require centralized financial support. Sources of funding could range from inter-governmental and industrial support to sales from commercial advertising on the database itself.

Proprietary Interests. Product manufactures may be reluctant to use the database as a mean of storing and disseminating their product information. They might be justifiably concerned with database security related to their products. General product information and methods for obtaining current, secure data directly will be made available in the database.

Data Quality. A loosely linked network, such as is anticipated for the global wood engineering database, is easily grown and pruned. Hence, the quality and longevity of any particular set of data is questionable. Procedures will be developed to assure users that the database is accurate and current.

Language. A global database will require that all nodes in the network support multiple–language access to their data.

POSITION PAPERS

A LOOK BACK AT RESEARCH NEEDS IN WOOD ENGINEERING

Richard J. Schmidt, M., ASCE[1] & Jay A. Puckett, M. ASCE[2]

Abstract

This paper takes a brief look back at the research needs workshop held by the ASCE Committee on Wood in 1983. The paper reviews the state-of-the-art as it existed in 1983 and summarizes the research needs at that time. The review is based primarily on the proceedings of the workshop. A brief assessment of research developments that satisfy those research needs is offered. This assessment is supported by searches of the open literature and conversations with selected experts in the specific areas of research interest that were examined. Overall, the 1983 research needs workshop can be considered a success in establishing clear direction for continued development and fostering cooperation among researchers.

Introduction

A workshop entitled: *Structural Wood Research, State-of-the-Art, Research Needs and Priorities* [Itani and Faherty, 1983] was held in 1983 in Milwaukee, Wisconsin. Research topics discussed at that workshop were grouped into eight categories:

I. Structural Materials — Lumber

II. Connections

III. Subassemblies — Walls, Floors, etc.

IV. Heavy Timber Structures and Bridges

V. Structural Materials — Panels

VI. Reliability Based Design

VII. Trusses and Manufactured Structural Components

VIII. Light-Frame Buildings

1. Associate Professor, Department of Civil and Architectural Engineering, University of Wyoming, Laramie, WY 82071.

2. Professor, Department of Civil and Architectural Engineering, University of Wyoming, Laramie, WY 82071.

During the workshop, panels of attendees reviewed state-of-the-art papers written by experts in their respective fields. Then the panelists discussed research activities and priorities, and prepared brief research need statements to accompany the state-of-the-art papers.

The objective of this paper is to take a brief look back to 1983 to review the state-of-the-art and the research needs identified at that workshop. Each of the research categories from the 1983 workshop is reviewed in the following sections. The state-of-the-art and the research needs identified by the session participants are outlined. An estimate of the research developments since the workshop, with respect to the vision established at the workshop, is offered. The primary assessment is based upon the reports written by the eight session chairs.

Each of the numbered sections that follows is divided into three subsections. The first two paraphrase the writings of others contained in the workshop proceedings. In the third subsection, the authors review research developments since the 1983 workshop. This review is based on a limited-scope literature survey on the Engineering Index (EI) from 1980 until 1996 and discussions with experts working in the specific fields as well as those with broad-based knowledge.

Although this is a limited review, it is sufficient to establish a perspective for the 1997 research needs workshop [Fridley, 1997]. This review is not intended to be comprehensive or exhaustive. To this end, the authors have limited literature citations to other literature reviews, research needs statements, and major research publications. No less than 1500 published articles related to wood engineering have appeared in the open literature since 1983. Clearly, a thorough review of this literature is not feasible nor is it warranted for the purpose of this work.

General Research Activity — Wood Engineering

An EI search was conducted for general structural engineering activity in the wood and/or timber area in the 1980's and the 1990's. The search query is *structur* AND (wood* OR timber*)* which indicates any form of the word *structure* and any form of *wood* or *timber*. The search in the 1990's database (1990–1996) yielded 658 records; 815 records were found in the 1980's. The number of records reported per year is illustrated in Figure 1. These records were found in journals and in conference papers and proceedings in Civil Engineering and Materials Engineering. In many of the following research areas, keyword searches were conducted using words associated with the research needs statements. The syntax for the queries follows conventional Boolean logic.

I.   STRUCTURAL MATERIALS — LUMBER

Research Needs (in 1983)

Galligan and Green [1983] wrote the state-of-the-art paper for structural lumber at the 1983 research needs workshop. Unlike many of the authors who wrote state-of-the-art pieces, Galligan and Green did not emphasize the state-of-the-art. Rather, they carefully outlined their perception of the research needs in their paper. Nevertheless, the state-of-the-art can be inferred from the detailed list of research needs that they developed. The following discussion parallels their contribution to the 1983 workshop.

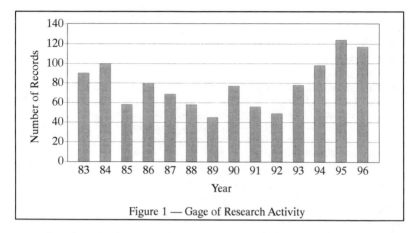

Figure 1 — Gage of Research Activity

Logging: Galligan and Green outlined many aspects of the state-of-practice in logging and cited a need for better in-field assessment of standing timber with respect to structural and laminating stock grades. They cite the need to detect incipient decay and to recognize the serious effects of juvenile and compression wood.

Sawing: The state-of-practice was one which principally emphasized volume yield with a lack of attention to (or interest in) minimizing the effects of structural defects. Little research had been conducted in this area. The need was cited to develop sawing methods for softwoods to target the structural integrity of the resulting product, rather than volume-based yield. The trend toward, smaller, rapid-growth timber was outlined as an issue. There was also a need to quantify slope of grain and other local distortions and use such information in sawmill trimming decisions.

Drying: The drying process can have adverse effects on the end product. The quality of dry lumber depends on the type of drying process, either restrained while kiln dried or unrestrained in ambient conditions. Irregularities and defects cause warping and the drying process degrades the material by "mechanical failure of the cell wall and between fibers caused by the rapid dehydration of the cellulose and lignin." Galligan and Green also note that some species are more adaptable to the drying process than are others. They cite research needs to: develop degradation prediction models adaptable to commercial kilns, study full-size lumber to relate internal checking to tensile and bending performance, develop methods to control warp and accelerated drying without significant material degradation, and develop quality control processes to assess the degree of chemical and physical degradation caused by the drying process.

Grading: Galligan and Green outline the basics of visual and MSR grading of lumber, but point out that a major concern is that no existing grading system efficiently relates the effects of incipient decay, failures of compression wood, or poor drying. They indicate that although MSR prediction is better than is visual, 40–60% of the strength variability is unidentified. They make very strong augments for improvement in assessing the structural properties of lumber and the need for advanced methods to make this assessment. Galligan and Green suggest that a "standard (probability-based) format for assessing the 'adequacy' of mechanical property assessment for commercial lots of lumber" be developed. They also suggest development of a method to identify incipient decay, compression wood, improper drying, a means of grading that explains more strength variation, and finally, more research on lumber properties related to use of lumber where several structural actions exist, e.g., beam-columns.

Fabrication and remanufacture: Lumber is used in a host of situations where it is placed within a final product unlike the original lumber form. For examples, these value-added processes include laminating, in the case of plywood panels or glulams, and connecting elements, in the case of trusses, etc. Preservative treatment is cited as an expanding area as well as the use of smaller stock which requires better understanding of structural adhesives. Galligan and Green cited the need for improved methods for "sampling, testing, and analysis procedures for assessing the adequacy of treated lumber based on full-size specimens in consumer-lot quantities." They also indicate the need for research in connections, notch or cut effects, and finally, failure mechanisms, quality control, and performance characteristics of composite lumber.

Transportation: Galligan and Green cited the need for more research on water-repellent coatings, wrapping procedures for effective protection, development of ASTM standards for assessing water penetration during transportation and storage, and finally, development of industry standards for acceptable water penetration and weather resistance.

Moisture Content: Several topics involving moisture content effects were cited as research needs. These included probability-based methods for analysis of moisture effects on specific lumber grades, the effects in lumber other than visual grades, such as MSR, and the effects in major assemblies (glulam and truss frames), including cyclic moisture conditions. Finally, Galligan and Green suggested moisture-induced stress evaluation in assemblies and studying the sensitivities to determine the area of greatest priority.

Temperature: The use of lumber in non-typical temperatures was reviewed. Galligan and Green suggested determining the "immediate" effect of temperature and its reversibility. They also recommended studying the effect of temperature on full-sized structural members. Finally, they suggested a review of structural uses where temperature and moisture may become a design problem.

Duration of Load: Galligan and Green cited limitations of existing research regarding the interaction of load duration and changes in moisture content and temperature. They outlined the high cost and significant time required to perform work in this area. They emphasized the need for work in the end-use environment for full-sized specimens, inclusion of more species, tests of subassemblies with mechanical joints, and basic research into the anatomy of failure to advance comprehensive models.

Chemicals: Galligan and Green stressed that treatment effects require attention. They stated, "it is a frustrating fact that while the use of preservatives is increasing dramatically in the United States in an effort to more effectively use wood in adverse environments, the treatments are proprietary and no published information is available on full-sized tests covering the treatment procedures that occur in practice." They cited Rowell [1980] who suggests that a systematic program for determining the strength loss mechanism as a function of environment be developed. Galligan and Green suggested studies on full-sized members that include the effect of treatment, moisture, temperature, and time. They also indicated the difficulty with drying processes related to treatment and cited the need for ASTM methods to address the above.

Biological Agents: The in-grade testing program was summarized and some of its shortcomings regarding species and mechanical properties were noted. Galligan and Green suggested a prioritization method for testing minor properties not addressed in the in-grade-testing program and recommended studies be conducted to address the importance of minor properties in contemporary structures. They also suggested research to establish the difference between "global" samples and consumer lot samples.

Summary of Research Needs (in 1983)

To organize, summarize, and expand the research needs identified by Galligan and Green, a summary statement was written for the session report. Four broad technical subject areas were identified: *processing, grading, end-use environment,* and *property assessment.* The report was a basic outline of suggested research. This outline is paraphrased below.

Processing: Processing needs addressed assessment of quality from tree to mill as a management tool and correlating the log quality indices to sawing decisions and to lumber quality (not just quantity). The changes in forest characteristics to small logs and modern sawmill technology were suggested as important. The assessment of drying and/or the effect of treatment on mechanical properties were cited as important.

Grading: NDT should gain emphasis to better assess lumber quality and to aid visual grading. More emphasis should be given to grading for end use. It was noted that "there is no shortage of high strength lumber, only a shortage of methods to identify it."

End Use Environment: Duration of load under cyclic ambient temperature and relative humidity are important and deserve attention. Load duration with respect to treatment, moisture, and temperature, as well as load interaction effects are important topics. A creep model is needed to include environmental parameters.

Property Assessment: Major properties were discussed relative to consistent apparent modulus of elasticity, which varies among test procedures. Other issues included: volumetric effects, performance-based tests, estimations of concomitant properties, combining teams of engineers and statisticians for proper analysis, dynamic properties, and interaction effects under combined loading.

Research Developments (since 1983)

The major advancement in the lumber area related to wood engineering (not wood science) has been the in-grade testing program. The program completed a national assessment and was implemented in the 1991 NDS [AF&PA, 1991]. Moody [1997] suggests new needs in this area are the quantification of properties of imported lumber and monitoring the property trends of existing lumber. Other areas noted are concerned more with wood and forest science issues and were not examined in detail.

II. CONNECTIONS

State-of-the-Art (in 1983)

The state-of-the-art review of mechanical connections for structural wood members was penned by McLain [1983]. Connection design is reviewed herein in terms of the type of fastener used to make the joint. Three major fastener types are common: dowel-type fasteners (including bolts, nails, spikes, screws, and staples), plate-type connectors (such as glulam rivets and the stamped plates used in wood trusses), and bearing-type connectors (including split rings and shear plates).

Joint Performance: In 1983, design of connections with any of these fastener types was governed by empirically-based practices and extrapolations of limited research data. These practices, which were adequate for decades, became unacceptable in light of increased sophistication and data needs of structural analysis software. A greater understanding of both the strength and stiffness of joints had developed. The call for more rational design procedures was also being made in order to provide a better balance between safety and economy in designs. Reliability-based methods that could provide more uniform levels of safety were sought for both member and connection design.

An analytical model for joint strength, now known as the European yield model, was proposed by Johansen [1941, 1949]. In the yield model approach, specific failure modes for dowel-type connections are based on material properties for the fastener and the wood. Specifically, the dowel-bearing strength of the wood and the flexural yield strength of the fastener are used with assumed stress distributions and the equations of equilibrium to predict the load capacity of a joint. This approach was interpreted and applied to US practice by McLain and Thangjithan [1983]. Hence, in 1983, the yield model approach to joint design was regarded as a promising research topic.

General stiffness models for dowel-type connections were not available. Numerical and experimental studies had been conducted to determine joint stiffness. However, these studies were limited in scope to just a few fastener types, joint configurations, and wood species. A major difficulty with estimating the load-deformation relationship for joints is setting a rational and consistent definition of the limiting load or displacement for service-level and ultimate states. Other complicating factors include the substantial differences in experimental performance of joints under monotonic versus cyclic loading and the absence of a generally applicable test method for finding joint stiffness and capacity. Finally, analytical models for withdrawal capacity or axial load-displacement response were unavailable.

Dowel-Type Fasteners: Design of joints with nails, spikes, and staples was based on the load at a deformation of 0.015 inches (0.4 mm). The load is found by empirical strength equations that were extrapolated from relatively limited experimental data. Relatively arbitrary adjustment factors were applied to account for material variability and load duration effects.

Lag and wood screws were also designed for withdrawal and lateral loading using empirical strength equations that depend on the diameter of the fastener and the specific gravity of the wood. The design equations yielded a withdrawal strength for a wood screw that was higher than that for a lag screw of the same diameter. No rational justification appears to exist for the difference. In 1983, there appeared to be little research activity in wood screws for structural applications, which might have been appropriate relative to the needs at the time. Some theoretical work related to lag screws was underway but studies of withdrawal resistance were cited as a particular need.

Design of bolts followed a similar method to that for screws. New developments in lateral loading of bolts, based on the yield model approach, appeared to be promising. There was still interest in improving the understanding of edge and end distance effects on bolted joint performance.

Plate-type Connectors: Design of metal plate connected (MPC) joints was, and continues to be, guided by recommendations of the Truss Plate Institute (TPI) and plate manufacturers. Design loads were taken from results of tests by the plate manufactures. Test procedures followed the guidelines of TPI and, in some cases, agencies that write the model building codes. There was some concern regarding the ability of the test procedures to replicate actual joint loading in the assembled structure. Hence, the usefulness of experimental strength and stiffness data for joint modeling was questioned.

Bearing-type Connectors: Design of split ring and shear plate connectors was based on published forty-year-old experimental work along with proprietary manufacturers' data. At that time, use of these connectors was declining due the high costs of fabricating the joints. Thus, little research interest existed in the US.

Research Needs (in 1983)

Research needs identified in the general area of connections included the following topics.

Design Procedures: Development of rational, uniform design procedures for mechanically fastened joints was a critical need. A unified theory for joint design would apply to different types of fasteners and would be verified with existing experimental data. Extrapolation beyond test results could then be performed with confidence.

Service Condition Effects: Evaluation of the influence of various service conditions on joint strength and stiffness was the second research need. Included in this topic are load duration, temperature, moisture content, cyclic environmental influences, manufacturing tolerances, fire resistance, cyclic and dynamic loading, and wood treatment effects.

Member-Connection Interaction: Issues of concern include joints that induce shear or cross-grain tension in members, joints designed to transmit moments between members, and joint stiffness effects on member and structural response.

Connections Between Structural Components: Examples include the joints between horizontal diaphragms and shear walls and those between roof trusses and walls.

Research Coordination Center: The objectives of the center are to serve the technology transfer needs of the industry and to coordinate research efforts in connections.

Research Developments (since 1983)

Perhaps the single greatest development in connection design has been the adoption of the yield model approach for dowel-type connections. This approach was originally developed in Europe for bolted wood-wood connections. Recent research has extended the method to include nails, screws, and metal side plates. The method is general enough to permit extrapolation to more unique connections using nonmetallic fasteners, such as fiber reinforced plastic rods and hardwood pegs. The method has become the basis of the dowel-type connection design provisions in the 1991 NDS [AF&PA, 1991].

McLain [1997] offered his views on several other developments in connection research. Service condition effects remain a concern but the perspective has changed. The issue now deals with how adjustment factors can be applied within the context of the yield models for connection design. Good progress has been made in the areas of repetitive and dynamic loading of connections. Effects of preservatives are also better understood than in 1983.

According to McLain, there is still no rational basis for member-connection interaction analysis, especially cross-grain tension and connection-induced shear. However, fracture mechanics methods do appear to offer promise of an analytical method. Also, the influence of intercomponent connection behavior on whole-building response is now recognized as a more critical issue than in 1983. Hence, it remains an important research topic.

Finally, the need for a research coordination center has been reduced by the explosive growth in communication forums and outlets that allow researchers to share their results. Growth in technical journals, international conferences, and computer networks all support greater communication and cooperation among researchers.

A search of EI was conducted with key words: *(connect* OR joint* OR fasten*) AND (wood* OR timber*)*. The search returned 221 citations from 1980 – 1989 and 96 citations from 1990 – 1996. In the 80's, much of the research focused on individual fastener types with nails seeing the greatest attention. Bolts, glulam rivets, and metal truss plates were roughly balanced in their citations. Shear plates appeared infrequently. In the 90's, attention focused on MPC trusses and international studies of split-ring and shear-plate connections. Studies involving seismic/dynamic/cyclic performance of connections became more common. Studies in reliability, semi-rigid joints, durability, and special-purpose fasteners also appeared.

III. SUBASSEMBLIES — WALLS, FLOORS, ETC.

State-of-the-Art (in 1983)

The state-of-the-art paper for subassemblies was prepared by Gromala and Wheat [1983]. Their paper included a broad discussion of the utility of the various subassemblies, a review of the important recent literature, and suggestions for continued research and incorporation of research findings into design practice.

Floors, walls, and roofs comprise the three primary subassemblies used in light-frame construction. Substantial experimental and analytical research had been conducted prior to 1980 to establish the basis for numerical models to represent floor and wall behavior. By the time of the workshop, system behavior of floors and walls was fairly well understood, but work in roof assemblies was relatively rare. Each subassembly was generally modeled independently of the others. For instance, the racking behavior of a wall model required different analytical considerations than did the bending behavior of a floor system. Also, for each subsystem type, a variety of models, each based on different behavior assumptions and modeling approaches, had been developed. The use of a "supermodel" to envelop all behavior mechanisms was technically feasible but its complexity was not warranted.

Floors: Successful floor bending models, including FEAFLO [Thompson *et al*, 1977], NONFLO [Wheat *et al*, 1980], and FAP [Foschi, 1982], incorporated load transfer mechanisms affected by fastener load-slip relations resulting in partial composite action, load distribution by two-way action and load sharing, and construction issues such as gaps between sheathing panels. The floor models were successful in representing experimental response of floors and provided valuable evidence in studies of system effects. That is, the numerical models demonstrated that the reliability of a floor system was higher than that of the materials used in its construction. Diaphragm behavior of floors was studied to a lesser extent than bending.

Walls: Racking is the primary load-transfer mechanism in walls and was modeled most often using energy methods that account for deformation of the fasteners, framing members, and sheathing. Mechanics of materials approaches, involving assumptions regarding wall deformation, were also used to formulate wall racking models. There was evidence that stiffness of shear walls was likely to be more important than ultimate strength, due to the high degree of deformation required in a wall in order to reach its strength limit. A review of wall racking models available at that time can be found in [Schmidt and Moody, 1989].

Roofs: Relative to floors and walls, roofs had received little research attention during the 1970's and early 1980's. Performance of individual roof trusses was well understood and a computer tool for truss design was (and still is) used in the truss industry. However, behavior of trussed roof systems was largely unknown. Analytical studies were rare but a few full-scale experimental tests had been performed. These tests showed that substantial load sharing exists in these systems.

Research Needs (in 1983)

Gromala and Wheat suggested that the many analytical models for subassemblies were near maturity and that a rational, orderly means be adopted to use these models to improve the design process. One suggested approach involved development of "assembly tables," similar in form to span tables, to guide selection of economical floor, wall, and roof systems that include system effects. However, this approach was not universally accepted by the professional community in that it was perceived as limiting the designer's options and creativity. The panel proposed additional research needs in this area, including the following topics.

Floors: Study human perception of motion and dynamic analysis. Study diaphragm behavior for systems with openings. Define realistic load criteria, vis-a-vis the standard 40 psf ($2 kN/m^2$) live load. Re-examine the strength and serviceability limit states, especially the strength limit states above service-level load. Continue development and evaluation of new floor systems that include new sheathing and framing materials.

Walls: The research needs for walls included investigations of connector properties, definition of limit states, development of simplified (non-finite element) analysis and design methods, improvement of test methods for racking, and investigations of cyclic performance.

Roofs: The greatest needs for subassembly research fell within the roof area. It was acknowledged that "no well-established analysis capability exists in this area." Presumably this statement applies to roof systems, rather than individual trusses. Hence, research needs focused on development of such analysis techniques, full-scale testing, and definition of limit states, load criteria, and design aids.

Research Developments (since 1983)

Research in static load response of floors and walls appeared to be nearing completion at the time of the workshop. The emphasis has since shifted towards serviceability, especially vibrations of floors, and performance of shear walls under seismic loading. Experimental studies of roofs were initiated soon after the workshop, followed by reliability-based modeling to study system behavior.

Dolan [1997] suggests that industry and code adoption of analysis models to improve design of floors and walls are not likely to occur due to the massive coordination effort and financial commitments required to achieve them. Simplified design procedures based on analytical models are not likely to be forthcoming due to the wide variety of construction methods and materials in use today.

Progress in roof system design is more likely. Reliability methods, discussed below, are leading to progress towards a better understanding of, and rational system factors for, MPC trussed roofs.

A search of EI was conducted for each of the subassemblies considered in this topic area. Keyword queries and the number of records found are listed below:

Keywords	1980–1989	1990–1996
wall* AND (wood* OR timber*)	118	49
floor* AND (wood* OR timber*)	71	29
roof* AND (wood* OR timber*)	101	41

The records pertaining to walls in the 80's focused on analytical models and testing. In addition, a significant number of records dealt with thermal performance and new sheathing materials. In the 90's, wall research dropped off, as expected. The focus changed to moisture penetration, new sheathing materials, and performance during natural disasters.

Floor research in the 80's involved little experimental research. Instead, topics included analysis models, fire, reliability, sound transmission, performance criteria, and framing methods. In the 90's, floor research continued in reliability analysis, system factors, fire performance, and vibrations.

Research in roof systems in the 80's included many studies in reliability. The focus tended to be on MPC truss systems. The search also produced records describing shell-type roof systems, glulam framed roofs, load distribution, and response to wind loading. In the 90's, the few available reports focused on performance during natural disasters, fire, reliability and system factors, duration of load effects, and system performance of MPC trusses.

IV. HEAVY TIMBER STRUCTURES AND BRIDGES

State-of-the-Art (in 1983)

The state-of-the-art report by Gutkowski and Williamson [1983a] provides the background to assess the developments in heavy timber structures and bridges. Gutkowski and Williamson also wrote an excellent state-of-the-art piece on timber bridges at nearly the same time [Gutkowski and Williamson, 1983b]. Since this time, significant work has been performed in this area. The state of the art in 1983 was one where engineering products were evolving from an earlier time when solid sawn elements were more widely used. An earlier research-needs report was developed in 1979 by the ASCE Subcommittee on Wood Research [ASCE, 1979].

Bridges: Gutkowski and Williamson cited recent developments that were significant advancements are that time. These included: product manufacturing, wood preservation, system approaches to design, and improved analytical and design methods. Specifically, glulam deck panels were replacing older plank and nail-laminated systems. The construction and service characteristics of these systems were being addressed in both the research and construction arenas [Sprinkel, 1978] and doweled joints were employed to improve bituminous overlay performance in the regions of the panel joints where cracking can be a problem. They cited the need for better cost data so timber deck systems could be better compared with competing systems.

Conventional, glulam-stringer bridge systems were noted as being rapidly constructed by crews of limited experience and the structures were performing well. Again, the problem of overlay cracking was noted.

Weyerhaeuser was cited for their innovation of panelized bridge systems. Here, the deck is attached to the stringers with an aluminum clip. No field drilled bolt holes were required and the necessary construction tolerance was ample. Hale [1975] had performed full-scale static tests to validate the design. Sprinkel conducted a press-lam bridge demonstration project in Virginia. Experimental and field-based serviceability characterizations were conducted. AASHTO distribution factors were conservative and hairline cracking was observed in the overlay.

Gutkowski and Williamson cited preservative treatments as important but did not elaborate on the state of the art in this area. Gutkowski and McCutcheon [1987] later conducted field-based observations that outlined the in-service performance.

Vehicle load distribution in bridges was and continues to be an area of interest, but only recent field studies were specifically cited in timber. Analytical studies were noted for bridges of other materials as well as recent work in composite deck action.

Long-Span Roof Member and Structures: The common theme cited by Gutkowski and Williamson — and in their assessment of the state-of-the-art roof systems — was stress perpendicular to the grain issues. Such cases arise in trusses and glulam bending elements that are tapered or curved. They cited lack of information on residual stresses from manufacture. They also cited numerous works by researchers in the US and Canada that address work in tapered element and arches.

Shell Forms: The recent construction of interesting shell forms was outlined with reference to several commercial and proprietary systems. Analytical details were not available and some comments were offered on possible improvements in analytical procedures to model composite action and joint fixity.

Research Needs (in 1983)

The research needs from the workshop are summarized in the following.

Loading: Dynamic behavior of bridges, heavy machinery and long-term effects were noted as important needs.

Experimentation And Product Development: Short- and long-term performance of connections under static and dynamic loads, fire resistance of heavy timber, including both analysis and empirical methods, a statistical database of material properties, and the effect on strength and stiffness of cuts, notches and holes were cited as primary concerns. The secondary interests were preservative treatment affects on strength after wet/dry cycles, stringer-deck connections, field testing of tutor arches, and more efficient glulam beam sections such as I, H, and boxes, post-tensioning laminated bridges, development of wood-steel composites, and capacity of members in horizontal shear.

Structural Analysis: Primary needs included rigorous analytical models considering orthotropic materials, load-sharing, discontinuities, semi-rigid connections, and nonlinearities, analytical studies of horizontal shear and torsional shear, improved failure criterion and a methodology for predicting torsional buckling.

In-place Performance: Research was suggested for procedures to evaluate existing capacity and methods for field repair of deteriorated and damaged structures. Secondary concerns that were noted included field performance of long-span timber structures, a controlled study of moisture content history of large timbers, and effect of field expedients.

Design: Primary research suggestions were development of moment connections for frames, re-evaluation of current allowable stresses for tension perpendicular to the grain, development of procedures for longitudinal bridge deck systems, design of guard rail systems per AASHTO, a unified design approach for non-prismatic members, and reliability-based design.

Top Research Needs: The research needs cited as "top priority" were outlined for emphasis; these include [Gutkowski and Williamson, 1983a]:

- Development of rigorous models for timber systems analysis,
- Short- and long-term performance of connections,
- Development of procedures for evaluating capacity of existing bridges,
- Dynamic excitation of timber bridges due to moving loads, and
- Fire resistance of heavy timbers.

Research Developments (since 1983)

Significant research has been performed in the area of static and dynamic analysis and performance of timber bridges. Much of this work has been performed as part of the timber bridge program. New bridge types have become common as a result of research conducted in the US and Canada. Such systems include stress laminated deck systems, glulam, and T- and box-sections. As a result of the developments in the bridge area, significant work has been performed by researchers at the Universities of West Virginia and Maine, at Iowa State University, and elsewhere. The FPL has contributed significantly to this effort. New funding is available to build demonstration timber bridges throughout the country and these efforts are often coupled with field observations, testing, and long-term performance assessments. Significant analytical work is coupled with the experimental studies. The work ranges from global load distribution effects to more local concerns addressing specific design/limit state assessment. Analytical work has also been performed to assess the load distribution in existing systems, e.g., plank decks. Software development has been perform by developers at the Universities of West Virginia and Wyoming.

Field-based studies have been conducted by researchers from Colorado State University and FPL. Long-term performance of decks, girders, and substructures has been assessed on the basis of relatively large samples.

An interview with Moody [1997] indicates that many of 1983 research needs have been met. Specifically, Moody indicated that there has been work in the area of rigorous models for timber system analysis, but that this has not had much impact on specifications at this time. The short- and long-term performance of connections work seemed to confirm the existing methods, except for composites. Moody indicated that a need remains for better assessment of the strength of existing bridges. Work is being done under FPL sponsorship on bridge dynamics.

To indicate the breadth of research addressed in this area, the authors searched EI with the keywords of *structural AND analysis AND (wood* OR timber*)* and 206 references for the 1990's were found. A close examination illustrated that most of the topical areas and research needs have been addressed. In the specific area of *bridge* AND (wood* OR timber*),* 120 records were found for the 1990's addressing areas of analysis, assessment of existing structural capacity, serviceability, and dynamics. New materials were used that employed wood and fiber reinforced plastics. Many of the papers were on stress-laminated structures. A query on *(shell* OR (long AND span)) AND (wood* OR timber*)* resulted on about 50 publications but only 20 that were relevant to structural analysis of shell, dome, or long span roofs. A query on *design AND bridges AND (wood* OR timber*)* resulted in approximately 70 records that address LRFD, load distribution, long-term performance, and new systems. A query on fire-related activity *fire AND structur* AND (wood* OR timber*)* resulted in 32 articles for the 1990's and 42 articles in the 1980's. This search illustrated considerable activity in the load bearing, treatment, and joints areas. Much of the work is reported by the international community. Finally, a search was posted to illustrate work performed in long-term performance of wood connections, since this was a priority area. The search for long-term or creep with connections resulted in no hits. So the search was generalized to *connect* AND (*long term OR creep) AND (wood* OR timber*)* and 97 records appeared in the 1990's.

V.   STRUCTURAL MATERIALS — PANELS

State-of-the-Art (in 1983)

O'Halloran and Youngquist [1983] wrote the overview of the state of practice in panel and structural composite products. They wrote a fine summary of the various panel products in use in 1983 and related these products to manufacturing and performance standards. Panel technology was reviewed, and testing and database management issues were elaborated. They outlined the use of structural lumber substitutes and structural composite components with respect to their histories and recent applications.

Research Needs (in 1983)

The research needs report was non-specific. The various groups presented their perspectives; these included US Forest Service, Canadian, university, and industry representatives. The research priorities were presented in six areas:

- Database development,
- Factors affecting design,
- Reliability-based design format,
- Fire,
- Construction methods, and
- Modeling.

It was suggest that the database should require/facilitate/store sound sampling over time, consistent testing, design properties, statistical analysis data, and opportunities for NDT correlation. The factors affecting design included in-service effects, treatments, and load duration including creep and creep rupture. A reliability-based design format was recognized as the method of the future. The panel also recognized a need for advances in assessment of fire performance of material, components and subassemblies, and improved construction methods. Finally, micromechanical modeling and component-level modeling to permit investigations without expensive pilot plants and other tests were outlined as priorities.

Although not discussed in the paper, the group indicated a "continuing need for education, not only in our universities but also in the ongoing education of the users in the design of wood-based composite products."

Research Developments (since 1983)

An EI search on *panel* AND (wood* OR timber*)* yielded 75 articles for the 1990's and 146 in the 1980's. As one would expect this range of articles was very large. The search was narrowed to include aspects of the database cited as a high priority; no reports were found.

An interview with Moody [1997] indicated that tremendous growth has occurred in the area of panel products in recent years. He was not aware of a panel product database as suggested above, and a literature search did not yield a citation in this area. Likely much of the data is held by proprietary interests. Moody indicated that load duration tests are being conducted and this work will be published as time permits. He indicated a need for work in the area of resistance of adhesives in panel products. Obviously, the need for reliability-based design is satisfied. However, construction innovations called for in 1983 seem to be placed at the wayside.

VI. RELIABILITY BASED DESIGN

State-of-the-Art (in 1983)

Reliability methods in wood engineering were reviewed by Goodman [1983]. At the time of the 1983 workshop, use of reliability-based methods was common in concrete design, emerging in steel design, and relatively unknown in timber design. Nevertheless, it was apparent that reliability-based methods had their greatest potential in timber. Presuming that the existing design methods produced safe and serviceable structures, the motivation for use of reliability-based design was to optimize use of a dwindling resource. Estimates suggest that up to one-third of the wood in structural applications could be saved without sacrificing structural performance. Goodman noted that this savings was immediately available, compared to any benefits that might be gained from improved forest management.

The major economic benefits that were expected from adoption of reliability-based design are the improved economy in use of materials with low variability (MSR lumber, glulams, and manufactured products) and in more efficient design of systems with load sharing. From a performance perspective, reliability-based design allows the selection of a level of reliability (a measure of safety) that is appropriate for a particular structure type and use. Also, the levels of safety for similar structures (or members) can be more consistent.

In 1983 reliability-based design for wood structures was not yet codified, and consequently not used in practice. However, there was substantial research activity in the area. Much of the research involved analytical and numerical studies that utilized past experimental data.

Research Needs (in 1983)

Research needs for reliability-based design included the following topics.

Member Behavior at the Limit States: Topics of interest included long columns under combined bending and axial force, effects of load duration, creep, and treatments and their interaction with moisture content variations, characterization of MSR lumber, minor species, and behavior in shear and tension perpendicular to the grain. Of particular interest were the issues of the required population size to predict system reliability and the potential for nondestructive testing to reduce data collection costs.

Connection/Member Interaction: A primary difficulty in using existing connection data to develop reliability-based design recommendations was the lack of standard test procedures. Specific research needs included characterization of limit state behavior (with adjustments for the usual load and environmental influences), development of experimentally verified mathematical models to describe connection limit states, and optimization of connection design and detailing relative to cost and target levels of reliability.

Single Member vs. System Reliability: Most past reliability research focused on single member behavior. Hence, little was known regarding the reliability of systems with load sharing. Specific research topics included characterization of loads for non-engineered structures, development of system testing procedures, and incorporation of time-dependent and environmental effects on system reliability.

Codification and Reliability-Based Design: In 1983, sufficient material data and analysis capabilities existed to permit codifying of reliability-based design recommendations. Key elements of this process are calibration of designs to existing structures and development of an educational program to accompany implementation of new code recommendations. Specific research topics included development of models for load duration effects and load characterization including duration of load cycles.

Research Developments (since 1983)

The 1983 workshop can be viewed as an unqualified success from the perspective of reliability-based design. The development of a reliability-based design standard and its attendant design values [ASCE, 1995a, ASTM, 1993a] for wood engineering marks a major milestone in this research area. A conversation with Bulleit [1997] helped identify other developments. Substantial progress has also been made in single member versus system reliability. System factors have been developed based on member type and material COV. Members with smaller COVs produce systems with smaller system factors. Remaining research needs include member behavior, especially beam-columns, and reliability of connections to improve the existing group-action factor and to study multiple-member connections. Bulleit prepared a comprehensive review of the literature in reliability-based design of wood structures. It has been published as Chapter 29 of the book edited by Sundararajan [1995].

The keywords: *reliability* AND (wood* OR timber*)* were used in a literature search of EI. There were 61 records during the 1980's and 40 records in the 90's that matched this keyword list. During the 80's, the largest percentage of the work related to reliability-based design (LRFD). Transmission structures and member behavior (especially damage accumulation) received considerable attention as well. Other topics of interest include connections, system performance, fire, bridges, and trusses. In the 90's, interest continued to focus on LRFD. Secondary topics included system performance, connections, member reliability, duration of load effects, and serviceability.

VII. TRUSSES AND MANUFACTURED STRUCTURAL COMPONENTS

State-of-the-Art (in 1983)

The state-of-the-art review in wood trusses and other manufactured structural components was written by Keenan *et al*, [1983a]. They outlined general needs for improved, automated and continual testing of wood for changing mechanical properties. They cited the need for more basic data and elaborated the expense associated with gaining the data necessary in the future. This general issue was followed by a discussion in the areas of roof trusses, floor trusses, wood panel web I-beams, glulam, and performance testing. Each of these areas is briefly summarized below.

Roof Trusses: Research had progressed along two parallel paths — prototype testing and analytical modeling. Suddarth [1969, 1983] stated that our analytical capabilities have outstripped our knowledge of the lumber and its behavior. Several analytical advancements and associated software are noted. The need for long-term material models and properties was cited as well as the need to model with a system approach.

Full-scale tests were cited as valuable and necessary, especially with respect to longer spans, where size effects and joint details may be different than their shorter span counterparts. Tests of 75 trusses by Keenan *et al* [1983b] and their results were briefly summarized and related to joint details, finger joints, and so forth. The authors cited a particular need for failure criteria for combined axial and bending moment with improved analytical tools for stress computations. They cited Zahn [1982] as a recent contributor in this area.

Floor Trusses: Keenan *et al* [1983a] cited recent work by Gromala and Moody [1983] where they estimated the residential floor truss market at 20% of all new floor construction. They cited Suddarth *et al* [1981a, 1981b] as a "major reference" in this area and that this work served as the basis of TPI-80. They indicate that a seven-year load-duration study will be completed soon (1983) and that research is being conducted on metal web systems in Canada. They outlined the possibility of improved performance in joint strength with metal web members, opening the possibility for effectively using high strength MSR lumber and composites for chord members.

Wood Panel Web I-Beams: Manufacturers have recently developed facilities and technology for prefabricated wood I-beams using solid sawn or laminated veneer lumber flanges and plywood or other structural panel materials for the web. Keenan *et al* [1983a] stated that "public research in the area of plywood web beams has been nearly nonexistent ... although they have conducted research and testing on their proprietary products." They suggested that it is now appropriate to conduct public research on the performance of these products.

Glulam: Forintek developed computer models for the strength analysis of laminated elements [Foschi and Barret, 1980]. A model was also used for fire endurance of heavy beams [Woests *et al*, nd]. Statistical simulations were under study to model strength and stiffness variability and their affect on MOR. Keenan *et al* [1983a] cited the need for improved in-plant quality control standards in the area of sampling and testing.

In system analysis, they cited a need to develop an improved model for axial load and bending moments, particularly where lateral torsional buckling is an issue.

Performance Testing: The need for more and improved testing to validate numerical modeling was cited as well as the need for automated means to measure deformation and strain data. A laser tool was suggested.

Research Needs (in 1983)

The workshop report succinctly outlines research needs. A list of these needs is given below.

Roof Trusses: Top chord stability of longer-span trusses, improved understanding of joint failures, combined loads on truss plates, creep and load duration with the affects of humidity and temperature, system behavior, axial and moment interaction, wood-based composites, fire performance and treatments, plate orientation, repetitive loading, and influence of exposure.

Floor Trusses: Standard test procedures for floor trusses that include wood/metal composite systems resulting in an ASTM standard, development of analytical models for wood and wood/metal floor trusses, long-term strength characteristics, and system behavior including deflection and vibration.

Wood Panel Web I-Beams: Long-term testing to include the effect of moisture and temperature cycling, development (with manufacturers) to include a combination of material and adhesive products, development of models for short- and long-term behavior, issues related to construction such as web openings, bearing supports and web stiffeners and attachment details.

Glulam: Fire endurance reliability formulation, Forintek model with existing data, tensile strength and stiffness of laminating lumber, new tension lams for higher grades, improved MSR techniques, improved reliability of tension proof testing, effect of quality control on reliability of end joints, developing lamstock from the alternative wood species, alternative test methods for submarginal glue bonds, effect of drying on resistance of lamstock, strength of glulam arches and columns subjected to axial and bending actions, long-term behavior, gluing of treated material, field identification of incipient decay, re-examination of strength of glue bonds, effect of width on strength.

Research Developments (since 1983)

The EI was consulted with the query *trusses AND (wood* OR timber*)* and approximately 190 articles illustrate work in all of the areas cited in 1983 as critical research needs. The articles include work on construction, performance observations, failures, semi-rigid joint modeling, fire assessment, creep behavior, system analysis, testing, and behavior. This query included articles on both roof and floor trusses. Floor systems included articles on service; strength issues included vibration and associated limit states. Regarding glue-laminated timber *(glue laminated OR glulam) AND (wood* OR timber*)* in the 1990's (19 records), the level of research activity has dropped off from the 1980's pace when 41 articles were posted. The 1980's saw significant activity that addressed many of the issues outlined in the research needs statement, including non-prismatic geometries, radial stress issues, and residual stresses.

Almost all areas examined for research needs indicate a need to study moisture effects on various aspects of behavior. A query of *moisture AND (lumber or structur*) AND (wood* OR timber*)* resulted in 52 and 43 articles, in the 1990's and 1980's, respectively. These papers addressed issues in the areas of strength and service behavior associated with lumber, panel, composite systems, connections, measurements, and adhesives as well as other areas.

Moody [1997] indicated that stability of roof truss top chords remains a problem, primarily while the system is being constructed. There has not been work on duration of load effect on trusses. There has been significant work in the area of analytical modeling and load testing of roof systems; work has been completed on axial force and moment interactions, and has been implemented into specifications. Moody indicated that extensive research on the effect of fire retardant treatments on roof systems has focused on their effects on the plywood sheathing. Results of research on the effect of repeated loading on full scale trusses will soon be reported, but little information is available on the effect of severe service conditions.

Goehring [1997] was consulted in the area of floor truss systems. He indicated the long-term effects were effectively addressed in the Illinois small home council 10-year study 81-1. Studies are progressing on service performance of floor systems, including vibration, but the traditional static deflection approach seems fine. Work has been performed and is currently being conducted to determine repetitive member factors to reflect system performance. Finally, it seems that many of the 1983 research needs have been addressed.

Moody indicated that work on prefabricated I-joists by individual manufacturers has formed the basis for ASTM D5055 [ASTM, 1994]. Little work has been performed on long-term behavior of systems with OSB webs and this remains an issue. Models for short-term behavior and creep are outlined in ASTM D5055. Finally, the manufacturer's guidelines for web openings are available and the industry is continuing to address this issue.

Moody indicated that progress has been made in several areas of glulam research. Much new information is available on alternate species. Advances have been made in modeling bending properties, including under fire conditions. The ASTM D3737 [ASTM, 1993b] and AITC 117 [AITC, 1993] standards include provisions for new tension lamination materials. He indicates that the need remains for better quality assurance procedures for fabricating end joints. There has been a lot of work with alternative species and fire resistance modeling.

VIII. LIGHT-FRAME BUILDINGS

State-of-the-Art

To summarize the state-of-the-art for light-frame buildings in 1983, Polensek wrote, "Presently, there is no modeling or analysis procedure that can predict the structural behavior of an entire, light-frame wood building as a three-dimensional system" [Polensek, 1983]. Light-frame buildings have continued to defy precise mathematical representation due to the complexity in their geometric design and the variability in materials and construction methods. Hence, their design was guided by subassembly performance, rather than three-dimensional structural behavior of the building system. In spite of historic good performance, increasing materials costs have lead to changes in traditional construction practices. Such changes can be expected to affect performance and their effects must be understood to assure that the safety of light-frame wood buildings is preserved.

The study of light-frame buildings can be broken into three categories: subassemblies, intercomponent connections, and entire building systems. Subassemblies are discussed in Section III. Hence, the focus of this discussion is on intercomponent connections and entire buildings.

Intercomponent Connections: Traditional connections (discussed in Section II.) have received substantially more research attention than intercomponent connections (joints between walls, floors, roofs, and foundations). Consequently, few recommendations exist for connection design and building codes provide no provisions for analysis. Nevertheless, intercomponent connections, as with connections in most structural systems, are often the critical link in the strength and safety of light-frame buildings.

Perhaps the lack of attention to intercomponent connections is due to the difficulty of establishing standard test procedures that replicate in-service conditions. Analytical and numerical models have been no more successful. The structural response of these connections is strongly influenced by material nonlinearities, interlayer and intercomponent gaps, construction and material variability, and dynamic behavior. These issues render modeling and analysis of intercomponent connections a computationally intensive proposition.

The finite element method does offer the potential for accurate and efficient analysis, if traditional program capabilities can be enhanced to represent the unique characteristics of light-frame structures.

Entire Building Systems: Existing codes contain no provisions for analyzing or testing wood buildings as complete structural systems. However, both experimental and numerical research studies have been conducted to study overall system response.

Experimental investigations are expensive and provide only limited data for a small number of structural parameters. Still, important findings related to composite behavior and component interaction have been made. The potential for full-scale testing of light-frame buildings is likely limited to that required for verification of general numerical models.

Theoretical studies, using the finite element method, are also somewhat limited due to the lack of special purpose software and the computational horsepower required to conduct a thorough study. Practical analysis models must include some method for homogenizing subassembly response into a super-element approach. Nonlinear analysis capability is essential to account for inelastic material response and intercomponent connection behavior.

It is not likely that comprehensive structural modeling will be a practical step in the design process for light-frame buildings. Instead, detailed models will find their application in the development of simplified, probability-based design methods.

Research Needs (in 1983)

The long-term research objectives in the area of light-frame buildings included efficient design of components and intercomponent connections through three-dimensional interaction, and safe design against natural disasters through whole-building analysis. The attendant research needs include the following.

Analytic needs: Three-dimensional analysis capabilities are needed for both strength and serviceability considerations. High priority modeling needs revolve around an assessment of the suitability and usability of existing programs, definitions of limit states, development of energy-dissipation models, performance of sensitivity studies, creation of a database for subassemblies, and development of models for intercomponent connections.

Experimental needs: Prohibitive costs limit the scope of experimental research needed to verify analytic models. Specific areas that require experimental studies include intercomponent connections, field studies of buildings under service and induced loads, natural disaster damage assessment, creation of a database for subassemblies, evaluation of internationally available information, and characterization of dynamic properties.

Loading needs: For the most part, loads on light-frame buildings are determined independently of the structural system. However, a few system-specific needs exist, including: load duration effects, simulation of loads for experimental procedures, and assessment of available load specifications.

Design needs: Design procedures and code development must rely on successful analysis of force distributions and deformations. In addition to the analytic needs above, there is need to reduce the complex, analytical models to simplified forms suitable for codification.

Research Developments (since 1983)

Research in light-frame behavior remained active for several years following the 1983 workshop, but has lessened in recent years. Some modeling efforts continue at Oregon State University and at the University of Wyoming, but experimental studies on conventionally constructed frames are rare. One reason is that the costs (in terms of both time and money) of detailed analysis outweigh the benefits gained by increased understanding of building behavior. It is simply easier and cheaper to add more sheathing to shear walls, add more tension anchors to sill plates, etc. when behavior questions exist. An exception to this rule is the manufactured home industry. In this case, economic and safety benefits of improved structural analysis can be high enough to warrant the costs of the analysis model. The new load criteria [ASCE, 1995b] for wind on low-rise, residential buildings has met a documented research need in this area.

A review of the literature in EI was performed with the search string: *((light* AND frame*) OR (three* AND dimension*)) AND (wood* OR timber*)*. This search produced 30 records in the 80's and 22 records in the 90's. These results might indicate a relative lack of continued research in this area. Many of the records focused on individual subsystems (roof, wall, floor) or on three-dimensional framed systems. However, several of the studies cited by Polensek [1983] and more recent reports on whole building models and tests did not appear. It is likely that the search string was not appropriate for its purpose. Nevertheless, research in light-frame buildings does appear to be waning.

Closure

The research areas cited as important in the 1983 research needs workshop [Itani and Faherty, 1983] were used for assessment of the state-of-the-art, research needs, and research developments. In many cases, experts involved with these areas were consulted for their views and input. These discussions were helpful and greatly appreciated. The primary purpose of this paper is to establish a perspective on research in wood engineering since 1983 and to lend relevance to the 1997 research needs workshop [Fridley, 1997].

Based on this brief review, it appears that many of the major research needs identified in 1983 have largely been met. Perhaps this can be viewed as a self-fulfilling prophecy. The research needs tend to follow the areas of active research at the time of the workshop. However, the workshop is important in documenting the state-of-the-art and the state-of-research at a point in time and in coordinating active researchers. Without these coordinated efforts, major technical advances, such as development of the LRFD specification for wood, would be unlikely to occur.

Finally, the Engineering Index can be located on the World Wide Web at the universal resource locator (URL):

http://cpxweb.ei.org

Readers will also be interested to know that the USDA Forest Products Laboratory maintains a web-based repository for their publications. Access to this web site is gained via the URL:

http://www.fpl.fs.fed.us/vcgi-bin/tpoicpdf.exe?Cmd=Query&Template=query3

Investigators may conduct reviews in specific topic areas, search for articles on various topics, and download documents to their computers.

References

AITC, 1993. *AITC 117-93 — Manufacturing Standard Specifications for Structural Glued Laminated Timber of Softwood Species,* American Institute of Timber Construction, 7012 South Revere Parkway, Suite 140, Englewood, Co. 80112.

AF&PA, 1991. *National Design Specification for Wood Construction (NDS),* American Forest and Paper Association, 1111 19-th Street, N. W., Seventh Floor, Washington, D. C.

ASCE, 1979. "Important Research Needs in Wood – As a Structural Material," *J. of the Structural Division,* Vol. 105, No. ST10, Oct., by the Subcommittee on Wood Research, ASCE.

ASCE, 1995a. *ASCE 16-95 — Standard for Load and Resistance Factor Design (LRFD) for Engineered Wood Construction,* American Society of Civil Engineers, 1801 Alexander Bell Drive, Reston, Va. 20191.

ASCE, 1995b. *ASCE 7-95 — Minimum Design Loads for Buildings and Other Structures,* American Society of Civil Engineers, 1801 Alexander Bell Drive, Reston, Va. 20191.

ASTM, 1993a. *ASTM D5457* —"Standard Specification for Computing the Reference Resistance of Wood-Based Materials and Structural Connections for Load and Resistance Factor Design," 1995 Annual Book of ASTM Standards, Section 4, Construction, American Society for Testing and Materials, Philadelphia, PA.

ASTM, 1993b. *ASTM D3737* — "Standard Practice for Establishing Stress for Structural Glued Laminated Timber (glulam)," 1995 Annual Book of ASTM Standards, Section 4, Construction, American Society for Testing and Materials, Philadelphia, PA.

ASTM, 1994. *ASTM D5055* —"Standard Specification for Establishing and Monitoring Structural Capacities of Prefabricated Wood I-Joists," 1995 Annual Book of ASTM Standards, Section 4, Construction, American Society for Testing and Materials, Philadelphia, PA.

Bulleit, W. M. 1997. Personal Communication with R. J. Schmidt, April.

Dolan, J. D. 1997. Personal Communication with R. J. Schmidt, February.

Foschi, R. O. and Barrett, J. D. 1980. "Glued-Laminated Beam Strength – A Model," *J. of the Structural Division,* ASCE ST(8), pp. 1735–1754.

Foschi, R. O, 1982. "Structural Analysis of Wood Floor Systems," *J. of the Structural Division,* ASCE, Vol. 108, No. ST7, pp. 1557–1574.

Fridley, K. J. 1997. *Wood Engineering in the 21-st Century, Research Needs and Goals,* Proceedings of a workshop held at Structures Congress XV, Portland, Or., April 13–16.

Galligan, W. L. and Green, D.W., 1983. Structural Lumber: An Overview of Research Needs," Structural Wood Research, *State-of-the-Art and Research Needs,* Edited by Itani, R.Y. and Faherty, K.F., ASCE, New York, NY.

Goehring, C. 1997. Personal Communication with Jay Puckett, March.

Goodman, J. R. 1983. "Reliability-Based Design for Wood Structures, Potentials and Research Needs," *Structural Wood Research, State-of-the-Art and Research Needs,* Edited by Itani, R.Y. and Faherty, K.F., ASCE, New York, NY.

Gromala, D. S. and Moody, R.C., 1983. "Research Needs in Structural Analysis of Light-Frame Wood Systems," *Proceedings,* IUFRO Conference, Madison, WI.

Gromala, D. S. and Wheat, D. L. 1983. "Structural Analysis of Light-Frame Subassemblies," *Structural Wood Research, State-of-the-Art and Research Needs,* Edited by Itani, R.Y. and Faherty, K.F., ASCE, New York, NY.

Gutkowski R. M. and Williamson, T. G., 1983a. "Heavy Timber Structures and Bridges," *Structural Wood Research, State-of-the-Art and Research Needs,* Edited by Itani, R.Y. and Faherty, K.F., ASCE, New York, NY.

Gutkowski, R. M. and Williamson, T.G., 1983b. "Timber Bridges: State-of-the-Art, " *J. Structural Division,* ASCE, No. 9, Sept.

Gutkowski, R. M. and McCutcheon, W. J., 1987. Composite Performance of Timber Bridges, J. *of Structural Engineering,* ASCE, Vol. 113, No. 7, July.

Hale, C. Y. 1975. "Field Test of a 40 ft. Span, Two Lane Weyerhaeuser Panelized Wood Bridge," Weyerhaeuser Report No. RDR-045-1092. Tacoma, Wa. May.

Itani, R. Y. and Faherty, K. F., 1984. *Structural Wood Research, State-of-the-Art and Research Needs,* ASCE, Proceedings of the Workshop held at The Marc Plaza Hotel, Milwaukee, Wisconsin, Oct. 5–6, 1983.

Johansen, K. W. 1941. "Forsoeg med traeforbindelser," (in Danish). Bygningsstatiske Meddelelser No. 2, Copenhagen.

Johansen, K. W. 1949. "Theory of Timber Connections," International Association of Bridge and Structural Engineering, Publication 9. Bern, IABSE, pp. 249–262.

Keenan, F. J., Suddarth, S. K., and Nelson, S. A. 1983a. "Wood Trusses and Other Manufactured Structural Components," *Structural Wood Research, State-of-the-Art and Research Needs,* Edited by Itani, R.Y. and Faherty, K.F., ASCE, New York, NY.

Keenan, F. J., Quaile, A. T., and Knight, J. 1983b. "Strength and Serviceability testing of Full Size Wood Structural Components," Proceedings, Structural Research, Canadian Society of Civil Engineering 1983 Annual Conference, Ottawa, Canada, June 1–3.

McLain, T. E. 1983. "Mechanical Fastening of Structural Wood Members — Design and Research Status," *Structural Wood Research, State-of-the-Art and Research Needs,* Edited by Itani, R.Y. and Faherty, K.F., ASCE, New York, NY.

McLain, T. E. and Thangjithan, S. 1983. "Bolted Wood-Joint Yield Model," *J. of Structural Engineering,* Vol. 109, No. 8, pp. 1820–1835.

McLain, T. E. 1997. Personal Communication with R. J. Schmidt, April.

Moody, R.C. 1997. Personal Communication with Jay Puckett, March.

O'Halloran, M. R. and Youngquist, J. A. 1983, "An Overview of Structural Panels and Structural Composite Products," *Structural Wood Research, State-of-the-Art and Research Needs*, Edited by Itani, R.Y. and Faherty, K.F., ASCE, New York, NY.

Polensek, A. 1983. "Structural Analysis of Light-Frame Wood Buildings," *Structural Wood Research, State-of-the-Art and Research Needs*, Edited by Itani, R.Y. and Faherty, K.F., ASCE, New York, NY.

Rowel, R. M., 1980. "Influence of Chemical Environment of Strength of Wood Fibers," Proceedings: How the Environment Affects Lumber Design: Assessments and Recommendations, US Forest Products Laboratory, Madison WI, May.

Schmidt, R.J. and Moody, R.C. 1989. "Modeling Laterally Loaded Light–Frame Buildings," *J. Structural Engineering, ASCE*, Vol. 115, No. 1, pp. 201–216, January.

Sprinkel, M. M., 1978. "Final Report - Evaluation of the performance of a Press-Lam Timber Bridge Performance and Load test After Five Years," Virginia Highway and Transportation Research Council, VHTRC 79-R26, Charlottesville, VA, Nov.

Suddarth, S. K., 1969. "The Engineering Design of Mechanically Fastened Trusses - A Review," *Wood Science*, Vol. 1, No. 4, pg. 193–199.

Suddarth, S. K., Percival, D. A., and Comus, Q. B., 1981a. "The Structural Performance of Parallel Chord Metal Plate Connected Wood Trusses," Final Report, HUD, Washington, D.C.

Suddarth, S. K., Percival, D. A., and Comus, Q. B., 1981b. "Testing and Analysis of 4x2 Parallel Chord Metal Plate Connected Trusses," Research Report 81-1, Small Homes Council, University of Illinois, Urbana, IL.

Suddarth, S. K., 1983. "The Changing Scene," Proceedings, *Wall and Floor Systems: Design and Performance of Light-Frame Structures*, Denver, CO.

Sundararajan, C., editor, 1995. *Probabilistic Structural Mechanics Handbook, Theory and Industrial Applications*, Houston, Texas: Chapman & Hall.

Thompson, E. G., Vanderbilt, M. D., and Goodman, J. R. 1977. "FEAFLO: A Program for the Analysis of Layered Wood Systems," *Computers and Structures*, VII, pp. 237–248.

Wheat, D. L., Vanderbilt, M. D., and Goodman, J. R. 1980. "Nonlinear Analysis of Wood-Joist Floors," Structural Research Report No. 26, Civil Engineering Department, Colorado State University, Fort Collins, Colo.

Woests, F., Bender, D., Schaffer, E., and Marx, C. n.d. "Fire Endurance Reliability Formulation for Heavy Timber Beams," Proposed Publication.

Zahn, J. J., 1982. "Strength of Lumber Under Bending and Compression," Research Paper FPL 391, US Forest Products Laboratory, Madison, WI.

Materials and Wood-Based Composites

Michael P. Wolcott[1]

Abstract

The last two decades has seen tremendous changes in wood materials, both structural and non-structural. These changes have reflected issues that range from material grading technologies through to engineered lumber products. Much of this transformation has been spurred by socio-economic influences like resource demand, cost of housing, and competing materials. Correspondingly, many of the innovations have been born in industry and influenced in large part by manufacturing technologies and materials economics rather than strict engineering needs or designs.

The objective of this paper is to collect and communicate some of the perceived needs in wood materials oriented research through the next decade. Being conceived prior to any formal planning process, this document is neither complete nor conclusive. Rather, it should be viewed as a point of reference and a place to begin discussions. This paper begins with a brief background covering the state-of-art in wood-based materials and components that are commercially produced and commonly used in construction. The major research needs are then organized in several broad categories that include: Materials Design and Production, Materials Performance, Materials and System Assessment, System Approach.

Background

Commercial composite materials and structural elements can be classified by their intended uses and constituent wood element that is used in production (Table 1). In wood construction, structural beam and plate elements are by far the most

---

[1] Associate Professor, Department of Civil and Environmental Engineering, Washington State University, Pullman, WA 99164-2910

common. Some molded composites are becoming available, however, these are used in non-structural applications like interior automobile parts and furniture.

Although early structural composites were produced from large wood elements, like lumber and veneer, recent trends have seen a strong influx of strand-based systems for both the beams and plates. This trend has been fostered by changes in resource and has increased the utilization of previously unused tree species and small size classes.

Almost without exception, wood-based composites have been developed to directly replace other construction materials. The earliest trend was the large-scale substitution of plywood sheathing for board sheathing. This application is again changing with the tremendous growth of OSB, primarily in the sheathing markets. In the last decade, the commercialization of I-joists have targeted large dimension lumber applications in floor and roof framing. Most recently, engineered lumber products have hit the 2x4 market; the smallest common commercial lumber size.

COMMERCIAL WOOD COMPOSITES				
	Beam	*Structural Plate*	*Non-Structural Plate*	*Molded*
Lumber	Glulam	Glulam	---	---
Veneer	Laminated Veneer Lumber (LVL)	Plywood	Plywood	Sporting Goods
Strand	Composite Strand Lumber (CSL)	Oriented Strand Board (OSB)	---	Chair Seats
Particles	---	Particleboard	Particleboard	Pallets
Fiber	---	---	Hardboard, MDF, Insulation Board	Door Skins, Interior Auto Components
Components	I-Joists Trusses	Structural Insulated Panels (SIP)	---	---

Table 1: Commercial wood-based composite materials ordered by use and constituent wood element.

Although wood-composites have produced dramatic increases in building efficiency. Light-weight and large sizes have both contributed to ease of application. The new finger-jointed and CSL wall framing lumber are aimed directly at improved use characteristics (i.e. straightness, consistency, etc.) that are declining from the decreasing quality of solid framing lumber. In the cases of beam elements, the improved engineering properties have changed building design primarily by increasing unsupported span lengths for roofs and floors. However, none of these materials have substantially changed the basic concept of light-frame construction. One exception to this rule is structural insulated panels (SIP's) which replace entire structural wall and floor systems. SIP's have seen their greatest success in the modern timber-frame market, as opposed to traditional light-framed buildings.

The newest trend in wood-based materials are hybrid composites that combine wood with synthetics (Table 2). Although not new in concept, tremendous advances are currently being made in both the science and commercialization of these materials. A major driving force for this recent interest has been the increased competition by synthetic materials in the traditional arena of residential construction. The major impetus for hybrid composites is the need to produce a material that handles like wood but performs in many ways like synthetics. These needs have been most evident in durable materials that are resistant to moisture and bio-degradation. The one exception has been reinforced glulam technology which aims primarily at the long span markets captured by LVL and CSL. The biggest current deficiency of these materials is cost. This one attribute may, however, be overcome by customer perception or code mandates.

COMMERCIAL HYBRID COMPOSITES	
Technology	*Application*
Synthetic Reinforcement	Glulam
Inorganic Bonded	Siding Roofing Wallboard Underlayment Tile-baker
Wood/Thermoplastic Composites	Decking Door and Windows Molding Contertops
Polymer Impregnation	Flooring

Table 2: Commercial hybrid composites that combine wood with synthetic materials.

Materials Design and Production

Resource-based issues will proceed to drive many of the research needs in design and production of wood-based composites. This trend will continue primarily from the increased percentage of small and under-utilized forest resources in the available cutting stock. In addition, the high volumes of short rotation southern pine and poplar plantation materials will increasingly become a major source of composite mills.

Interest in recycling post-consumer wood waste increased during the 1990's from a decreased availability of sawmill residues in the western US and an increased consumer interest in recycled materials nationwide. Some corporations have made significant efforts to utilize this new resource. A number of particleboard and MDF mills now supplement their raw material supply with recycled chips. However, supply quality still plagues the industry and much of the upcoming challenges lie in materials sorting and handling to produce a consistent, clean supply.

The use of recycled material in structural applications remains in the early development stages. Recycled timbers are currently in large demand for niche markets like timber framing. However, appropriate grading technologies and standards are needed for reuse and remanufacture of solid wood components on a large scale. Poor primary processing characteristics from low moisture contents appear to be the primary challenges for recycled use in structural wood composites.

An increased emphasis on hybrid composite technologies will be needed to expand the performance envelope of wood-based materials. The volume of residential housing markets is enormous compared to those currently realized by most synthetic materials, especially reinforcing fibers. An increased use of synthetics in combination of wood-based materials should drive cost improvements for these components. However, increased use will only come with improved economics and performance of the hybrid materials. Research efforts should strive for more efficient use of the synthetic components. Technologies that improve resistance to moisture and bio-degradation with reduced dependence on biocides are particularly important. In addition, novel processing methods will assist in both economics and roles for synthetics.

Materials Performance

Many of the concerns or deficiencies in wood-composite performance can be categorized as durability issues. Specifically, durability can be viewed as (1) creep and duration of load (DOL) performance, (2) moisture absorption and the resulting degradation in material properties, and (3) biological degradation.

Creep performance of many non-veneered wood composites has been shown to be extremely poor in laboratory studies. However, these results contrast strikingly to the absence of actual creep related failures in the field. Research is needed to address the actual load histories of materials and representative testing regimes. In addition, it is critical to develop accelerated test methods that produce meaningful data for both engineering analysis and product performance.

Composite materials abound for a variety of interior applications, however, many of these materials are difficult to treat for exterior use. The common preservative treatment for consumer wood products is CCA which actually decreases the moisture related weathering performance of wood. There is need to expand the treatments or product performance towards moisture and decay durable wood composites.

As wood engineers, we often concentrate attention on the structural components of a building. However, non-structural materials that are used in doors, windows, siding, trim, and roofing often comprise the largest cost of a residential structure. These materials are foremost in the minds of the owner since it is these materials that they contact daily. In addition, these non-structural components often have strong influence on the reliability and longevity of the structure they protect. The court records stand testimony to our need to continue research towards durable and reliable wood-based composite products for these exterior applications.

Wood has flourished over the years as a construction material primarily from its ease of use and widespread availability. These attributes have continued to drive much of the success for engineered wood composites like LVL and CSL which can be higher cost than standard steel sections in many applications. These same parameters, however, have driven much of the disfavor of solid wood framing materials and new interest in steel framing. Research needs to be directed towards property requirements of CSL framing material.

Materials and System Assessment

Non-destructive evaluation (NDE) techniques are currently well established within the wood lumber and composite industries. Many of these systems have a high cost which are then passed onto the material cost. As such, the use of MSR lumber is fairly restrained to pre-engineered materials. Research is needed for low-cost NDE that can be widely used for both composites and solid wood. These techniques should be flexible enough to accommodate in-place evaluation of materials. In contrast to the classical deflection techniques that are often used for lumber evaluation, stress-wave timing and ultrasonics have this flexible capability. Similar systems can provide data that can be used in property assignment and load assessment with similar methodologies.

Many problems associated with wood-based materials in construction can be traced to problems with construction practices. Currently, these practices are difficult to inspect since many of the materials are covered at key inspection times. In addition, current inspection standards are qualitative in nature. NDE techniques that can assess the general integrity of building systems would provide invaluable information influencing perceived material performance.

System Approach

Current wood-based materials have been designed as a direct substitute for solid lumber products. Opportunity now exists to coordinate material and structural system design to optimize performance. This effort is particularly evident in research topics like floor system vibrations where connector performance and subfloor-joist interactions significantly influence structural performance.

Connector behavior with composites is an often overlooked area for wood-based materials. Here, design can be focused on both novel connections and composites that optimized for traditional connections.

Conclusions

Composites will continue to play an increasing role in building construction. With this increased reliance on new materials, research must be directed to understand and control long-term behavior and durability issues. Hybrid composites may provide some novel approaches to these problems if cost can be moderated. Attention must be given to non-structural materials that protect building systems. Affordable NDE techniques that can be used for both materials grading and structural load rating are needed. A systems approach to materials and structural design will provide large gains in building systems.

Connectors and Fasteners: Research Needs and Goals

Thomas E. McLain[1], Member ASCE

Abstract

In the late 20th century, research and information transfer on structural connections between and to wood members have emerged as a critically important needs. Advances in technology and in understanding the responses of structural systems to a range of loadings have challenged our knowledge base for structural wood connections. This paper reviews previous efforts to identify connections research needs and priorities since 1983. The author suggests challenging needs for knowledge and education in four broad areas: a) *connection concept*, where new ideas in connectivity can solve problems and create opportunities, b) *connection design*, where a stronger empirical or theoretical basis for consistent design guidance is needed, c) *connection installation* where construction practices can enhance or negate design assumptions and safety levels, and d) *connection service performance*, where service-related changes in performance are largely unknown.

"A structure is an assembly of connections separated by members."

Introduction

Although this statement is thought by some to be tongue-in-cheek, designers, contractors and insurance investigators have all seen some truth in it over the past decade. The ease and relative low total cost of making connections to and between wood members is a key strength of timber as a structural material. Connection simplicity was an important component in the expanded use of light-frame wood structures to meet post war housing needs. In North America, this low cost and relative simplicity, coupled with greater industrial and regulatory interest in new component materials, engendered little research interest in connections until the 1980's. For the

---

[1]Prof. of Timber Engineering and Dept. Head, Dept. of Forest Products, Oregon State University, Corvallis, OR, 97331 USA.

most part, public research has focused on behavioral, safety and code issues with generic fasteners. Private or proprietary efforts have concentrated on labor savings and connections with proprietary materials. Most research has been very applied and was generally a reaction to an identified problem. Almost all of this research in the US was empirical and relatively few test replications were made. As a result the principal connection design standards in North America are largely founded on research done over the period of 1920-1955. This knowledge base has served us well as evidenced by few wholesale failures attributed to connections and by the generally successful performance of most connection types .

However, changes in construction materials, construction practices and engineering analysis methods have put new demands on our knowledge of connection performance. Research since the early 1980's has highlighted the connection as a critical component in structure response to some loadings. This has been especially evident with structure performance in wind and earthquake disasters over the past decade. As a result, there has been more focused attention by design and regulatory authorities on expected loadings, design standards and construction practices. This attention has surfaced new challenges and needed improvements in engineering practice. Recent experiences have also highlighted the importance of fabrication and installation to overall quality and performance of the constructed product. Also, there is some evidence that traditionally non-engineered structures may be held to different design standards in the future than has historically been the case.

Other major factors highlighting connection importance has been a rapid expansion in the use of new engineered wood materials in the marketplace and the continuing development of innovative structural systems. Although viewed as wood substitutes, engineered wood composites often pose unique connection challenges that may not be supported by the current research base, and which often accentuate the need for care in installation. The development of technology and innovation leading to panelized roof systems, portal frames, space trusses, domes, manufactured housing, prefabricated light-frame components and many others pivots on connection performance for success. Structural design practice has also changed with the problems and opportunities offered by computerization and increasingly sophisticated analysis tools. Our North American experience is generally mirrored by similar activities in Europe, Japan, New Zealand and Australia. As a result of all of the above there is greater realization of the role of connections and renewed interest in a more fundamental understanding of fastening mechanics.

The purpose of this paper is to set the stage for a workshop session that will consider needs and goals with connection research in the 21st century. The state of research knowledge is not reviewed here and the interested reader is encouraged to review McLain (1984), Foliente and Zacher (1994) and Task Committee (1996) for that information. In the past twenty-five years there have been several attempts to develop consensus on research needs and goals with connections. Those are important precedents to the 1997 workshop and a review of them is a helpful starting place.

1983 Structural Wood Research Needs Workshop
        The 1983 conference in Milwaukee was attended by invitees who represented a broad cross-section of researchers, engineers, code officials and industry representatives. There was a separate session on connections as well as others on subassemblies, light-frame buildings, and heavy timber construction that also surfaced connection research needs. These are summarized here with some commentary, but the interested reader is encouraged to review the conference proceedings (Itani and Faherty 1984). Only those research recommendations that explicitly pertain to connection issues are captured below.

From the Connections Session

- Development of rational, uniform design procedures for mechanically fastened joints. Included here was a need for standardization of testing and the development of a more theoretical underpinning for current design standards. Also envisioned were the special information needs required by true reliability-based design methods.

        Significant progress was made with some of these needs in the past 14 years, largely driven by an upgrading of the *National Design Specification for Wood Construction* (ANSI/AF&PA 1991) and by the development of a complementary design standard in LRFD format. Some of these efforts are summarized in AF&PA (1992) and McLain, et al. (1993). A defining change was to move the design basis for laterally-loaded dowel-type fasteners from an empirical foundation to a more theory-supported yield model approach (characterized by European yield models (EYM) predicting capacity at distinct failure modes). This move capitalized on an existing European research base and may be a significant step toward international code harmonization. This new base, however, required additional research support, especially for North American species and construction practices.

- Evaluation of the influence of various service conditions on joint strength and stiffness. Research needs were identified to assess the influence of:
    --load and time,
    --temperature and relative humidity, especially cyclic changes,
    --manufacturing tolerances and installation variabilities.
    --fire,
    --repetitive and dynamic loads,
    --wood treatments.

        These needs remain largely unmet but some progress has been made. As discussed later, many items on this list are seen by the author as priority needs for the future. The conversion of North American codes highlighted weaknesses in research knowledge and testing standards. One key issue that emerged is the need to predict the future capacity or assess present residual capacity in connections subject to a variety of service conditions. Nondestructive and destructive evaluation techniques have been explored but no generally accepted theoretical foundation for degradation has emerged for many service effects. One example is with load and time. At present, our design standards assume that the duration of load reduction for connections is that same as for component properties. Limited research in Europe suggests a smaller effect for long term loads and work in the US suggests limits to increased strength for short duration transient loads. A significant gap in our knowledge is with the interaction of fabrication tolerances and number of fasteners on the performance of multi-fastener connections. Research since 1983 has heightened our understanding of the importance of fabrication details on multi-fastener connection capacity. We know that the theoretical base for our current US design standard is flawed, but there is currently no strong evidence for an alternative.

- Analysis of the interaction between member and connection. Included here are issues related to reductions in member capacity as a consequence of the presence of a connection. Shear and tension perpendicular-to-grain are common concerns. Another similar issue is with the design of joints to transmit moment or provide end fixity.

Moment connections have been the subject of considerable work in New Zealand and Europe. US work has focused on the performance of proprietary connectors. Work outside of the US has attempted to quantify potential shear and tension reductions for some connection types. There has been limited effort in the US which may suggest that either efforts to proscribe connection details or conservative design standards have minimized concern.

- Design and detailing of connections between structural systems.

Intercomponent connections have emerged as a critical issue with structural performance, especially in wind and seismic load conditions. Modeling the actions of those connections and developing improvements in design has seen some attention. More will be needed as we move toward developing engineered 3-D wood structural systems or to support deemed-to-comply standards for conventional construction practices.

- Establishment of an Information and Research Coordination Center for collecting research knowledge and coordinating research efforts globally.

No substantive effort has been made here and research is still scattered and fragmented. That probably won't change, especially with government disinvestment in central research infrastructures. However, communications around the world have improved immensely in the past 15 years and the need for an information center may be lessened. Hopefully, this workshop will contribute to meeting this communications need.

Session on Subassemblies, Walls, Floors, etc.

- Connector properties for sheathing-to-frame and intercomponent connections.

Considerable effort has been made with this area over the past 15 years with various load-slip models and analytic tools that consider nonlinearity in connection response. Most work has been with nails. Limited information has emerged for adhesive connections and for connections between wood and steel or concrete components.

Session on Light-Frame Buildings

- Models of intercomponent connections, experimental tests of intercomponent connections, determination of dynamic properties, damage limit states and other factors.

Many factors were not identified in 1983 as specific connection-related issues in this session. However, it was recognized that connections played a key role in system modeling and performance. None of the connections issues in this session were specifically identified as high priority research issues. In retrospect, a high priority need to identify limit states for damage due to lateral and uplift loads implicitly includes connections.

1992 International Workshop on Wood Connectors

The Las Vegas workshop consisted of a series of research state-of-the-art presentations and summaries of design code treatments from several international perspectives. Unlike the 1983 Conference the 1992 workshop was focused on connection issues alone and the audience was heavy to research with a strong mix of foreign delegates. Discussion groups followed presentations to identify needed research. Bjorhovde and Suddarth (1993) summarized the identified research needs in the proceedings. A slightly condensed list of identified needs is shown in Table 1 for reference. No priority was assigned to the items on the list. It should be noted that this list, like any similar product, reflects the concerns of the day and the nature of the individuals present. Although the conference was well attended, the group may not represent the breadth of those whose input for such a list should be sought. Nevertheless, there are many very important long and short term issues on the list.

California Workshop on Timber Structures Under Seismic Loads

This research needs workshop focused on timber structures and seismic loading. Because connections tend to dominate structural seismic response, the proceedings of this workshop offer some contemporary insight which we should consider. The interested reader should review the overview papers in the proceedings, especially Foliente and Zacher (1994). From the workshop summary, the following connections-related research recommendations emerged:

- Establish a set of guidelines for cyclic testing of wood joints, ... is a high priority need.

Assessing the performance of connections subject to cyclic or dynamic loads is presently complicated by a lack of agreement on test standards and the type of information that is most helpful in assessing expected connection performance in a structural subsystem or component. Dynamic testing is inherently more complex and this could be viewed as another chapter in the well-known dilemma of relating lab tests to field performance. A further complication is the need for test standards which also support and enable the development of relatively complex models to predict structural response.

These needed guidelines must also be supplemented by a clear set of performance indicators and standards for special-purpose connections such as shearwall hold downs and diaphragm attachments.

- Duration and rate of loading effects, fatigue and cumulative damage.

Need for research in this area has been highlighted by several groups. As we become more interested in repetitive loads or large motion effects, the weakness of our research base with these effects becomes more problematic. Cyclic testing of structural systems shows us that performance and connection-related failures are not well predicted by our current empirical knowledge base for single fastenings.

Some Discussion

There are striking similarities between the 1983 and 1992 lists which may indicate that many problems remain despite a decade of research attention. My review of the literature for the past twenty years suggests that, with some exceptions, our research efforts have largely been fragmented and that we have not recovered from a long period of limited investment in connections research. Our experience with revising the 1991 allowable stress design standard and in crafting a new LRFD standard served to confirm our ignorance. That process also highlighted many relatively short-term applied research needs, some of which are described later. A significant additional factor is that our building design, analysis and performance needs have changed in the last decade requiring even more knowledge. All indications are that the next decade will see additional change and greater interest in engineering traditionally non-engineered structures. This suggests that the 1997 Workshop will be able to surface a rich pallette of opportunities and that prioritization may be difficult.

It will be easy to develop a list of connection research needs. In another page or so, I will use my author's license to offer some of mine and those I solicited from others. It may be helpful to the participants preparing for the workshop (or those reading afterward) to think about research, or knowledge needs in the overall context of the design and building process. We could separate engineered from non-engineered or semi-engineered structures in our thinking at this point, although I hope that the two are close. Again, taking some license, it seems to me that we could view connections research needs and potential questions in the context of the following four stages:

1. *Connection Concept*---where we are presented with an opportunity or problem relating to connections between or to wood members. Could be thought of as part of the design process but design generally considers some predetermined alternatives and creative activity in making one or more of them work. Let's think about this phase as creating an opportunity or solving a problem. The impetus for innovation could be a new material, new technology, building configuration, design or cost constraint, labor challenge, material shortage, need for greater efficiency, new market potential, architectural challenge, etc.

There are likely to be both long and short term needs in this category. More applied and directed research by the private sector will address market opportunities and capitalize on changes in technology. Some additional research will be needed in response to a changing regulatory environment. Changes in construction technology and the integration of non-traditional materials will drive research efforts in some sectors. A major challenge may be with the need for guidelines and standards for testing and evaluating connection systems under realistic in-service loading regimes. Our present fragmented set of national and local standards are inadequate if we are truly interested in moving to performance-based specifications for connections and structural systems in the future. This is a major challenge which will require considerable effort for the next decade if significant improvements are to be made.

Wood is a fascinating composite material with an intricate set of internal efficiencies in its morphology. One is tempted to think that tree physiology and wood anatomy may hold some opportunities for improving our ways of joining members. Biomimetics may offer some interesting long-term research ideas to improve upon our principal centuries- old mechanical fastening systems. Adhesive technology seems to have progressed to where reliable connections are fabricated in the manufacturing plant. Are there barriers to the use of adhesives for other applications and venues? What are the functional barriers to fully efficient connections?? What is the next innovation in fastening that might have the same engineering and market impact as the punched tooth metal plate?

2. *Connection Design* — in engineering design we need the ability to predict future performance under a set of anticipated loadings and to satisfy a variety of needs with economy, safety, constructability, aesthetics, etc. Trying to improve design practice always results in a list of specific research needs to develop information on which to base some engineering judgement. At a more fundamental level we need to understand the process of load transfer and energy absorption through the connection and how to optimize those for selected connection types. If we are to develop a true reliability-based design standard then we will need to estimate expected variability in the installed product and to be able to assess safety across a range of different connection alternatives that may have different load transfer mechanisms. Serviceability issues with connection systems will add additional design complexity and expand our list of information needs.

Realistic and comprehensive test standards will be needed to support new design specifications for performance and to allow for rapid entry and safe use of innovations in the marketplace.

At a more fundamental level, a stronger theoretical basis for design would be welcome for many existing connection types, both generic and proprietary. Improved prediction of future performance will require significant advances in our understanding of the complex relationships between connection mechanics and the service environment.

3. *Connection Installation*--installation methods and practice are known to influence the service performance of many connection types. Yet, for the most part, that influence is not quantified and often not explicitly considered in design practice. Ostensibly, some component of a design "safety factor" accounts for that level of ignorance, but the true effects and level of variability are largely unknown.

A good case in point is the known influence of fabrication tolerances on the performance of connections with multiple, large diameter bolts. While a theoretical load distribution may be assumed for each fastener by the designer, it is the fabricator who determines the actual distribution. For some connection orientations where load may be directed perpendicular-to-grain, a nominal variation in hole location may result in cracking. Getting our arms around the multiple bolt/fabrication problem will be a challenging project.

New technology in labor saving systems and the expansion of prefabricated engineered components and subsystems offer new challenges. A major concern is with inspection and quality assurance in the constructed product. Engineering and human factors research will be needed to improve compliance, establish realistic quality standards and performance criteria that can be quantified and evaluated.

4. *Connection Service Performance*---as noted at earlier workshops, the influence of service conditions, particularly combinations of conditions, is often unknown. Acknowledging that performance may degrade with time is sometimes difficult, especially if our design and evaluation systems don't allow for that reality. Moisture, temperature, time, load history and material characteristics interact in

complex ways in connections that may not be predictable from member or component performance. For some connection types in solid wood we have good information and performance history on which to base our expectations. For newer materials we often assume they act like wood in the absence of other information. That may or may not be the case and each material will require specific evaluation. We are learning, however, that even for wood there are surprises with connections such as the likelihood of significant mechanosorptive creep effects on deformation and strength (e.g. Lu and Leicester 1994).

We know that connection performance may degrade with time in some environments and conditions. That degradation is largely not quantified but new NDE technology may give us the ability to do so and thus enable estimates of residual capacity and reliability. This could prove to be a rich area for future research. Again test standards that help estimate the effects of service environment could be very helpful in avoiding future problems. Developing cost-effective means of assessing durability will also be a challenge technically and politically.

All-in-all, changes in connection performance in service may be one of the most important future research areas, especially given increasing interest in assessment of our large inventory of existing wood structures.

An Author's List

As promised, here are some research areas and topics that I see as needing attention. This is not an inclusive list, nor is it in any priority order. It is offered as a way of helping focus the workshop discussion. The words are mine, but credit is due to many collaborators for their contributions and validation. I especially value input from Greg Foliente, CSIRO Australia; Phil Line, AF&PA; Dave Pollock, Washington State University; Karen Colonias, Simpson Strong-Tie Co.; Larry Soltis, USDA Forest Products Lab; Dan Dolan, Virginia Tech and Dominique Janssens, Structural Board Association who responded to my request for their thoughts and perspectives. This offering is grouped into two components; the first is a series of major research areas where broad advances are needed and the second is a collection of more targeted research needs to fill gaps in our knowledge.

■   *Major Areas of Research*

Expansion or Supplementation of Connection Mechanics Theories and Reconciliation of Inconsistencies. The recent change in design of dowel connections from a empirical basis to a European yield theory foundation provides a more rational basis for setting design values for a variety of generic dowel-type fasteners such as nails, screws, dowel, bolts and lag screws. Like most major changes this conversion was made with sufficient, but necessarily limited data. EYM has been extensively researched in Europe and is founded upon some key behavioral principles that apply to the vast majority of connection designs. North American practice and materials do differ somewhat, however, and codification of some provisions was made despite some inconsistences between test observations and theory assumed behavior. Some of these relate to the selection of the 5% diameter offset yield strength as a design point. For many fasteners this point is experimentally unique and is a reasonable approximation of the onset of fastener yield. For others, such as perpendicular-to-grain connections and those with dowel greater than 25.4 mm in diameter, fracture may be observed at or before the 5% yield point is reached. For small diameter fasteners, this experimental micro cracking is not generally a concern. For larger fasteners the results may be more serious and related more to fracture mechanics than yielding phenomena. That is one reason behind the diameter limitation in current US design codes. In any event, it is important to provide a strong theoretical basis for design over the total breadth of design space. That requires an improved understanding of connection mechanics and the integration of several theory bases to explain and predict performance. This improved mechanics base will be critical in setting concomitant design provisions for service conditions, and extending supporting theories to other fasteners which also have dowel-like behavior in shear transfer (e.g. timber rivets, staples, punched metal plates).

A separate, but related, need is for a theoretical basis for strength or deformation prediction for connections with bearing devices such as shear plates, spike grids, split rings and the like. However, I judge this to be a lower priority than for dowel-type fasteners.

Guidelines or standards for testing and evaluating connections or joining systems under realistic load effects. Our current connection test standards are woefully inadequate to meet the information challenges with 21st century structural design. The need for cyclic or dynamic loading information is a good example, but incorporating the reality of many possible failure mechanisms into our test standards is of equal importance. The issue is that our test standards do not consider a variety of single and multiple loadings which might be expected of a connection in service. Some recent discussions in Australia (see Foliente and Leicester 1996) serve to highlight similar issues we find in revising our North American design codes and with rationally opening the marketplace for connection innovation. If we are truly interested in moving toward performance specifications and standards then our test methods and procedures need to be revised to enable that reality. Considerable research will be needed to support bold moves, but the beginning steps might be fairly easy to take.

A related need is for a rational and consistent method of converting test results to design values which considers the breadth in characteristics of various connection types and variability in test data. Both serviceability and strength are important.

Load distributions in multiple fastener connections. Enough has been said already, but this issue transcends most types of fasteners and a variety of fastener actions. Dynamic response in multiple-fastener connections will be a special challenge and opportunity. This is a good area for some international cooperation, especially if we can gain consensus on testing and theory.

Dynamic performance of fasteners and connections. Fatigue, strength and stiffness degradation, energy dissipation and ductility information is needed for a wide variety of fasteners and connections. Test and data standards will be a critical first step. Linking connections performance to systems performance will also be a challenge.

Assessing and predicting in-service changes in connection or connector performance. This is a common thread thru all previous workshops and is a major effort considering all possible fasteners and service conditions. I suspect that innovation in developing a theoretical or semi-theoretical basis for degradation will be the key to future knowledge and in avoiding huge experimental programs that may be difficult to fund. NDE of connections could be a key component to assessing and managing degradation.

This research area includes critically needed understanding of mechanosorptive effects and load-time interactions in connections where local bearing stresses may be very high or where friction may play a key role in residual connection capacity. In my opinion, these should be high priority needs.

■ *Targeted Research To Fill Gaps In Knowledge*
Dowel bearing strength of fastened materials: properties of wood-based and non-wood materials including plywood, OSB, particleboard, gypsum, insulation, plastic, aluminum, concrete, etc; interaction between diameter and grain or machine direction; fastener geometry (esp. noncircular) and surface effects on bearing strength.

Dowel fastener material properties for design; appropriate F_{yb} for large diameter fasteners, relationship to wire or bar properties prior to manufacture, nondestructive evaluation in situ.

Experimentally verified design procedures for laterally loaded and axially-loaded connections between wood to concrete or wood to fiber reinforced plastic (FRP) components.

Evaluation of and design provisions for head pull-through of axially-loaded fasteners (nails, screws predominately, but bolts also) from wood and composite panel materials.

Lateral and withdrawal design values for wood, sheet-metal and decking screws fastening composite panel materials under various service conditions.

Explore the relationship between lateral load capacity and depth of penetration with driven and turned fasteners, especially under variable service conditions.

The influence of spacing or other geometry requirements and connection performance. Most unknowns are with smaller diameter driven or turned fasteners.

Group action factors for wood-to-concrete connections. In the short term, the need is for recommendations consistent with our current elasticity-based system. Longer term, this needs to be a component of more comprehensive research on multiple fastener connection mechanics.

Rational means of predicting performance (and designing) mixed fastener connections, especially with connections tailored to meet several concurrent engineering objectives such as strength and ductility.

Effective means of repairing and evaluating field connections.

Literature Cited

ANSI/AF&PA NDS-91 National Design Specification for Wood Construction.(1991). American Forest and Paper Association. Washington DC. 132 p.

Bjorhovde, R. and S.K. Suddarth (1993). "Research needs for wood connectors and connections" in *Proceedings of International Workshop on Wood Connectors*, Las Vegas, NV 1992, pp 147-148. Forest Products Society, Madison WI, 148 p.

Foliente, G.C. and E.G.Zacher (1994), "Performance tests of timber structural systems under seismic loads" in *Analysis, Design and Testing of Timber Structures Under Seismic Loads, Proceedings of a Research Needs Workshop*, G. Foliente, ed., Univ. California Forest Products Laboratory, Richmond CA, Sept 1994, pp 21-86.

Foliente, G.C. and R. Leicester (1996), "Evaluation of mechanical joint systems in timber structures", *Proceedings of the 25th Forest Products Research Conference*, CSIRO Division of Forestry and Forest Products, Clayton, Victoria, Australia, Vol 1, Paper 2/16, 8 pp.

Itani, R and K Faherty, ed. (1984) *Structural Wood Research: State-of-the-Art and Research Needs*, Proceedings of the Workshop, Milwaukee WI, October 1983. American Society of Civil Engineers, Washington, DC., 210 p.

Lu, J. and R. Leicester (1994), "Deformation and strength loss due to mechanosorptive effects" in *Proceedings, 1994 Pacific Timber Engineering Conference, Gold Coast Australia.*, Vol 2, pp. 169-172.

McLain, T.E. "Mechanical fastening of structural wood members--Design and Research Status" (1984), in *Structural Wood Research: State-of-the-Art and Research Needs"* Proceedings of the Workshop, Itani, R and K Faherty, ed., Milwaukee WI, October 1983. American Society of Civil Engineers, Washington, DC., pp 33-68.

McLain,T.E., L.A.Soltis, D.G.Pollock, Jr. and T.L.Wilkinson.(1993). LRFD for Engineered wood structures--connection behavioral equations. *J. Structural Engineering*, Vol 19, No 10, pp. 3024-3038.

Task Committee on Fasteners of Committee on Wood, American Society of Civil Engineers (1996), *Mechanical Connections in Wood Structures*, ASCE Manuals and Reports on Engineering Practice No 84, American Society of Civil Engineers, New York, NY, 231 p.

Table 1.   Research Needs Identified in 1992 International Workshop on Timber Connectors. Condensed from Bjorhovde and Suddarth (1993).

General Needs:
• Communication: definitions, procedures, international harmonization of codes, research, and grading rules. Uniform tolerances with engineered construction components.
• Funding needs and priorities
• Better interaction between researchers and practitioners; improved continuing education.
• Standard statistical procedures and measures of reliability for LRFD or RBD development, uniformity in databases

Code Development:
• Non-dimensionalized design codes.
• Test standards for testing and evaluating proprietary connections.

Materials:
• Standard methods to assess properties and variability in common nails, material embedment strengths, yield and ultimate strength.
• Improved reliability in properties through grading techniques.

• Effects of cyclic moisture, stress concentrations, brittle fracture phenomena.
• Design and analysis methods for tension perp in connection materials.
• Material and adhesive durability, finger joint configuration.

Fasteners and Fastening Methods:
• Installation problems with lag screws, bolts and screws.
• Short and long-term strength and energy absorption characteristics of connectors.
• Embedment strength in dissimilar materials.
• Allowable strength discontinuities between similar fasteners in common sizes
• Withdrawal design values for mechanical fasteners.
• Improved assessment methods for interaction between adhesive and mechanical fasteners.
• Adhesives and protection systems for improved finger joint performance.

Connections:
- Modeling connections for improved correlation with test results. Models for hanger connections and multiple bolt connections. Analytical models and design criteria for large bolted connections and for multiple bolt joints.
- Deformation limits for capacity calculations. High ductility connections for braced framing.
- Service effects including: creep, load duration, moisture cycling, fire, durability.
- Moment connections: materials elements details, modeling, stiffness and ultimate strength, cyclic load response.
- End, edge and spacing requirements for nailed and screwed connections.
- Stitch bolt connections.
- Analytical procedures and design criteria for full-member finger joints.

System Connections:
- Modeling of system connections for improved correlation with tests,
- Test methods for complete joint systems for all load effects.
- Intercomponent connection systems
- Extreme and cyclic loading characteristics including energy absorption, ductility demand and supply, creep and other duration effects.

Special Connection Types:
- Nail Plates: models for strength and local buckling effects; stress concentration effects.
- Adhesive Dowel: ultimate strength modeling, beam-to-column connections, wood and concrete, seismic response
- Glulam rivets: shrinkage effects in sawn lumber; energy absorption characteristics.

Fabrication and Construction
- Durability, tolerances
- Field evaluation of decay and structural performance; effects of preservative and fire retardant treatment.
- Effect of over-driving mechanical fasteners, use of non structural spacer blocks.

Natural Hazard Mitigation
Bradford K. Douglas, P.E., MASCE

Abstract

Analysis and substantiation of building code provisions, including those for wood-frame conventional construction, are being required by regulators, insurers and property owners. As a result, recent regulatory activities have required new buildings in high hazard areas to be engineered in an effort to reduce property losses associated with natural hazards. While these activities increase the performance of individual elements in the structure, the effort lacks a consistent point of reference to measure and ensure improvement in overall building performance.

Determination of acceptable relative levels of risk to society must be developed to understand and improve the relative relationship between engineered design and conventional construction. Performance-based codes would provide the ideal mechanism for making these changes.

Introduction

Damage to structures from natural hazards such as hurricanes, floods and earthquakes, has resulted in assertions that current design and construction practices are inadequate. In the aftermath of Hurricane Andrew in August 1992 and the Northridge Earthquake in 1993, the scrutiny of conventional wood frame construction performance was raised to critical levels. Regulators, insurers and property owners have begun to demand that all building code provisions, including those for wood-frame conventional construction, have an engineering basis. As a result, recent regulatory activities have required new buildings in high hazard areas to be engineered. The intent of such activities is to reduce the property losses associated with natural hazards. While rational, these activities lack a consistent point of reference to measure and ensure improvement in overall building performance.

Engineered Design versus Conventional Construction

Wood accounts for more than 95% of the material used in framing residential structures in the United States. It also accounts for a large part of the framing for small commercial and light industrial buildings. A significant portion of wood frame construction utilizes conventional construction provisions included in the model building codes. These conventional construction provisions offer several advantages to stakeholders in the building process including ease of use, simplicity, uniformity in construction, and reduced cost. However, "unacceptable" damage to buildings built using conventional construction provisions has resulted in an accelerated move toward engineered design, especially in high hazard areas.

Engineered design provides a higher level of assurance that connections and members will have sufficient resistance to design forces. However, engineered design generally increases the cost of construction and requires better training and supervision of the construction process.

The actual level of risk to a structure designed and built to conventional construction or engineered criteria is difficult to quantify with a high degree of confidence. In the engineered design process, actual loads on a structure or element have been replaced by a system of design loads which, presumably, envelop the structural actions on the structure or element. Likewise, approximating damage to a structure or structural system based on the performance of a single element is difficult.

In general, it can be presumed that engineered design has a lower relative level of risk than conventional construction. The relative level of risk can be compared using the current system of design loads as the basis (see Figures 1-3). It is interesting that general agreement exists on acceptable levels of risk (or performance) for wood members resisting gravity loads. However, agreement does not exist on connections or the design of structural elements resisting wind and seismic. Without some analysis and comparison of the actual loads to the design loads, controversy will continue to exist.

Level of Risk

The current relative level of risk associated with conventional construction can be weighed against the relative level of risk associated with engineering design. This analysis would need to consider several issues including historical performance of conventional construction, uncertainty in loads, variability in resistances and acceptable levels of performance.

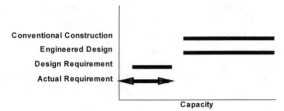

Figure 1. Relative Floor Joist Capacities

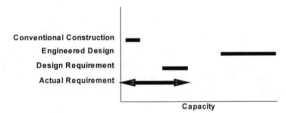

Figure 2. Relative Heel Connection Capacities

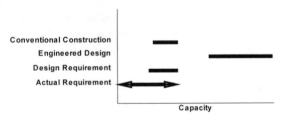

Figure 3. Relative Shearwall Capacities

Given the _relative_ level of risk can be determined, society must determine the acceptable levels. An effort to determine a system of acceptable relative levels of risk must be a cooperative effort between public officials, regulators, the design community, insurers, builders, and owners.

Implementation

If performance-based adjustments to current design procedures are deemed appropriate, modifications must be made to accommodate a system of relative levels of risk. Performance-based codes provide a mechanism which allows the incorporation of acceptable levels of risk. Recently, the NIBS Building Seismic Safety Council (BSSC) established multiple performance levels for seismic evaluation and retrofit of buildings in _NEHRP Guidelines for the Seismic Rehabilitation of Buildings, (FEMA 273)_. In this document, performance levels for structural and non-structural systems were defined. These guidelines, currently being balloted by the BSSC, define the following performance levels for structural systems:

a. Operational Level - Backup utility services maintain functions; very little damage.

b. Immediate Occupancy Level - The building receives a "green tag" inspection rating; any repairs are minor.

c. Life Safety Level - Structure remains stable and has significant reserve capacity; hazardous non-structural damage is controlled.

d. Collapse Prevention Level - The building remains standing, but only barely; any other damage or loss is acceptable.

Conclusion

Regulators, insurers and property owners have begun to demand that all designs, including wood-frame conventional construction, have an engineering basis. As a result, a number of regulatory activities have required new buildings in high hazard areas to be engineered. The intent of such activities is to reduce the risk of loss associated with natural hazards. While rational, these activities lack a consistent point of reference to measure and ensure improvement in overall building performance.

While the actual performance requirements of a structure, system, or element may not be quantified, the relative performance requirements can be developed using current design loads and engineering design algorithms. Using relative performance requirements, relative levels of risk can be developed.

Fire Performance Issues

Steven M. Cramer[1] and Robert H. White[2]

Abstract

The worldwide movement toward performance-based building codes is prompting the need for new computational methods to predict fire endurance of wood assemblies. Progress in the past twenty years in understanding fire endurance of individual solid wood components has been achieved in many different countries. The greatest opportunity for major advance in fire research is the development of computational fire endurance models that incorporate heat transfer, thermal degrade, and structural analysis algorithms for not only single components but multiple-component assemblies subject to standardized and natural fire scenarios. Full-scale test programs will also be needed to verify computational techniques and further develop thermal degradation theories.

Why Fire Research is Needed

Fire is a special design consideration addressed to minimize the risk of failure modes including structural collapse. Fire is not a loading condition in the traditional structural sense of applied forces, but instead an environmental condition that can have a dramatic impact on load carrying capacity and structure safety. The primary objective of fire resistant structural design is to maintain structural integrity during a fire for a sufficient period so that occupants may safely evacuate, fire fighters may safely extinguish the fire and to minimize property loss. This design process includes confining any potential fire with strategically-placed barriers and fire stops. Research on fire resistant design and construction in the United States appears to have diminished in recent years, although internationally it continues to be actively researched. In the U.S. fire resistant design receives much less research attention than similar efforts related to earthquake resistant design or the response of structures to wind events such as hurricanes. Can it

---

[1] Professor of Civil and Environmental Engineering, University of Wisconsin-Madison, 1415 Engineering Drive, Madison, Wisconsin 53706.

[2] Supervisory Wood Scientist, USDA Forest Service, Forest Products Laboratory, One Gifford Pinchot Drive, Madison, WI 53705

be that fire resistant design in the U.S. is more than adequate, thus explaining the low level of research activity?

Generally available statistics show that 4000 to 5000 civilian deaths and 8 billion dollars of property damage result from approximately 600,000 structure fires in the United States per year (World Almanac 1997). Forty-three of these fires representing about 0.01 percent of all structure fires accounted for about 18 percent of the estimated structure fire dollar loss in 1995 (Badger 1996). Both the cumulative small house fires and the large loss fires are causing significant life and property costs. In contrast over the past 10 years, average yearly death rates from earthquakes and hurricanes (in the U.S.) have been less than 1 and 70 respectively. Clearly, the potential for severe human life and property loss exists from a single extreme earthquake (as evidenced recently in Kobe, Japan) or a hurricane. Nevertheless, recent statistics suggest that risk to human life per year in structure fires is higher than for earthquakes and hurricanes. Why then, do we not devote more research effort to fire resistant designs?

The fire performance of new engineered wood components continues to be challenged and questioned (Brannigan 1988, Corbett 1988, Grundahl 1992, Malanga 1995, Schaffer 1988). Some in the fire protection community have strongly questioned the fire performance of these components because they are less massive and thus less able to resist a rapid temperature rise than comparable solid wood components. Sometimes, prohibitions and restrictions in engineered wood component use have been proposed, but without a strong scientific basis to back their claim.

Fire-resistant construction practices for buildings in the United States have been controlled by prescriptive standards specified in building codes. Inclusion in the prescriptive standards has depended upon full-scale fire endurance testing of assemblies under ASTM E 119 or other similar international standards. These full scale tests are expensive, and slowly, accepted calculation procedures are being recognized by the codes as an alternative (White 1995). Prescriptive standards are convenient in that they free building designers from technical knowledge of fire. Because the construction details are prescribed (such as the minimum width of an exit corridor, etc.), there is often little opportunity for innovation in design without facing the daunting task of changes to the code. As a result, the prescriptive methods can lead to a perception that once the prescriptive requirement is met, what can be done has been done, and no further efforts or attentions are needed. Some believe that fire safety can be best improved by simply increasing enforcement of existing prescriptive requirements.

In contrast to the prescriptive code environment currently prevailing in the United States, performance-based fire safety regulations in building codes are being investigated and adopted in other countries. Performance-based code requirements present an objective and needed minimum result, as opposed to dictating construction details for achieving an unstated objective and an implied result as in prescriptive codes. The performance-based codes empower the designer with the possibility of a wide array of solution strategies for providing fire safety (Bukowski and Babrauskas 1994) with the possibility to provide better or equal performance at less cost and thus achieving a competitive advantage. However, such an array of solution strategies only comes from an understanding of fire performance and development of reliable calculation procedures to predict fire performance.

New Zealand moved from a prescriptive to a performance-based building code several years ago (Buchanan and Barnett 1995) and Australia is rapidly moving in that direction for fire safety (Clancy, et al. 1995). Japan and the United Kingdom have been working toward performance-based codes since 1982 (Tanaka 1994; Bukowski and Babrauskas 1994). Since 1994, Swedish building regulations BBR 94 and BKR 94 have been performance based and Norwegian building regulations have been undergoing review with the objective to develop performance-based design. Eurocode developments are also headed toward offering the option of performance-based requirements (Kruppa 1996, Konig 1994). The authors have observed that in those countries where performance-based codes have been adopted or are about to be adopted that fire performance research is vigorously pursued to meet the demand for technological innovation that the performance-based codes reward. Prescriptive codes in several countries prohibited wood frame construction greater than two stories. The adoption of performance-based codes has fostered wood construction innovation such that three and four-story wood construction is now being accepted.

In the United States, building code officials acknowledge that we are beginning an increased migration from prescriptive to performance-based standards (Zeller, 1997). The wood products industry has identified participation in the fire aspects of performance-based code development as a top priority. As emphasized by Fewell (1997), the development of building codes in the United States is distinctly different from other countries but developments in the past five years have now led toward a single set of uniform model building code documents. While the end of this process is not clear, it seems to lay the ground work for major advances such as the eventual adoption of performance-based code provisions. The National Fire Protection Association points out that the issue is not if or when we will practice performance-based design, but how performance-based design can be supported (Puchovsky 1996).

The motivations for conducting fire resistant research are thus clear. It is likely that the United States will follow the evolution of code development and eventually move toward performance-based codes. The need for fire research knowledge and predictive tools in this environment will be urgent for designers. Puchovsky stating the position of the National Fire Protection Association: *"The completion of a performance-based design requires a technical understanding of fire safety principles, followed by the application of proven engineering methods and calculations. This process relies heavily on science and engineering."* As stated by Tanaka (1994), "fire models are indispensable to a performance-based design system...." Although, fire models have a role even in a prescriptive code environment as an alternative or supplement to standardized fire endurance testing, the main motivation for model development is the eventual application of the full flexibility of fire models with performance-based codes. The increased knowledge and model development needed to exploit performance-based codes will not spontaneously occur. Research must advance hand in hand and preferably ahead of the changes toward performance-based specifications. Failure to do so may put the U.S. construction industry at a competitive disadvantage compared with construction in other parts of the world.

Human life and property losses resulting from structure fires can be reduced as fire endurance is better understood and new construction practices are developed. Popular engineered wood structural members will be recognized for either the fire safety that they offer or fire-resistant weaknesses will be revealed, understood, and addressed with development of suitable fire endurance systems before catastrophic experience. This research may expose fire-resistant weaknesses in some products and designs but may also open new markets by showing acceptable fire endurance performance and gaining new code acceptance. Fire endurance research serves to sort fact from perception and can guide the development of economical fire safe designs.

Overview of Research Topics

The primary areas of fire research related to structural engineering are:

1) Fire growth
2) Thermal degrade
3) Fire endurance

The context and emphasis of these areas in fire research, and of subtopics within the areas, have changed considerably in the past ten years. Previously, the major emphasis was on understanding the fundamentals of fire growth. Less of an effort was directed toward fire endurance. In the past 10 years this trend has reversed and considerably effort has been directed toward understanding fire endurance and developing fire endurance models. Fire growth research offers the opportunity to measure and simulate the thermal conditions associated with actual fires. Thermal degrade research involves measuring and characterizing material behavior based upon thermal conditions and fundamental knowledge of wood and gypsum. Fire endurance research uses knowledge gained from the two other research areas and principles of structural analysis to predict the load carrying capability of wood components and assemblies under fire conditions.

Fire Growth Modeling

Fire growth research has the objective to improve predictions of heat and smoke release rates, temperature development, and products of combustion (SFPE 1995). Regulations based on fire test methodologies for such "reaction to fire" performance criteria affect the use of wood products and other combustible materials. Fire growth models are critical for evaluating the risks to life safety if a fire should occur. Generally, this type of research has not been conducted in the context of structural engineering nor incorporated in structural models or structural design. This research is important to understanding the nature of structure fires and ultimately it will play a complimentary role in structural models that predict fire endurance. Debate continues on how structures behave in standardized test fires such as those in ASTM E-119 versus natural fires (König and Norén 1995, Buchanan and Thomas 1996). Computer programs containing mathematical fire models, once verified, will allow a multitude of realistic structure fire scenarios to be examined for a design.

Related to fire growth are the topics of combustion toxicity and sprinklers. Combustion toxicity received tremendous attention during the 1980's but research has recently decreased in this area (Hall 1996). Yet, toxicity is the principal mechanism causing fire-related deaths. While outside the scope of structural engineering research and general fire endurance issues, combustion toxicity is a continuing research topic within fire safety. Automatic sprinkler systems provide options in building design pertaining to allowable floor areas and use of combustible materials. The use of the new engineered structural components has raised issues pertaining to the proper placement of the sprinklers.

Thermal Degrade of Wood Materials, Protective Sheathing and Connections

Understanding and predicting wood material behavior during and after pyrolysis is key to ultimately developing fire endurance models. This research consists of two interrelated steps:

a) heat transfer modeling of the transient thermal gradients occurring through the wood material and possible air zones around the wood as influenced by protective layers of sheathing and connections,

b) material characterization of the chemical changes associated with the exposure of wood to elevated temperatures.

Heat transfer models developed to simulate the influence of a protective layer of gypsum sheathing have been reported (Mehaffey et al 1994 and Clancy et al 1995). While these efforts provided a critical first step, modeling protective sheathing performance in a fire for variety of realistic construction scenarios (including the effect of construction joints and the ultimate failure of the gypsum sheathing) is very complicated and requires further study despite the recent progress (Takeda and Mehaffey 1996 and Clancy 1996). The possible break down of the protective sheathing as influenced by structural deflections is a problem that potentially limits the application of current fire endurance models (Cramer and White 1996).

At the time of the 1983 ASCE Workshop on Structural Wood Research (Itani and Faherty 1984), the action of most mechanical fasteners exposed to fire was unknown. The problem is complicated by the fact that the connectors act as thermal conductors and large temperature gradients exist in the wood surrounding the connector. Work on nail connections (Norén 1996) and metal plate connections (Shrestha et al 1995, White and

Cramer 1994) has provided some information. However, considerable research is still needed to define connection behavior. Better knowledge of thermal degrade of wood will facilitate understanding the behavior of different connection methods in wood structures exposed to fire.

Research on the thermal degrade of wood material has been conducted at several levels. Some models separate wood degrade into a two-material system consisting of charred wood and residual wood (Imaizumi 1962, Lie 1977, Woeste and Schaffer 1981, and Bender et al. 1985). This requires knowledge of char rates (White and Nordheim 1992, White and Tran 1996) and includes an empirical thermal degrade factor for the residual wood. Knudson and Schniewind (1975) modeled the wood section as a composite of small elements with distinct properties. King and Glowinski (1988) considered the section as a series of layers and used transform section analysis to account for the resulting property differences. Other approaches treat the section as a homogenous cross section but compute a net property degrade across the section by accumulating the time of exposure (Cramer and White 1993, Shrestha et al. 1995). Schaffer (1973) examined the degrade characteristics of residual clear wood. More recent efforts have been directed at examining thermal degradation of full-scale lumber (Norén 1988, Shrestha et al. 1995, Lau and Barrett 1997). The fundamental roles of pyrolysis on creep and the role of time of exposure have been introduced in previous investigations but work remains in advancing these theories to a practical level that can be applied to full-scale lumber and wood composite components.

Fire retardant treatments and coatings offer another aspect to thermal degrade research but are beyond the scope of the structural engineering research (White 1984). Generally these treatments suppress flame spread but do not retard the thermal degrade in engineering properties.

Increasingly engineers and architects are faced with the need to evaluate and rehabilitate a wood structure following a fire. Information is very limited and applicable primarily to heavy timber members (Freas 1982). The need for research on the thermal degrade of wood properties also applies to the residual strength that remains after exposure to elevated temperatures.

Fire Endurance of Wood Structures

Fire endurance research consists of testing or computational procedures by which the survival time of a timber structural component or assembly is measured or predicted. This area differs from thermal degrade work in that fire endurance involves the combination of thermal modeling, thermal degrade, and structural calculations to assess survival time. If a testing approach is taken, numerous tests are needed to allow isolation of various effects and to allow interpretation of test variability. Testing programs are also needed to serve as verification of developed models. Currently, a large full-scale wood assembly fire test program is underway in Canada (Richardson and McPhee 1996).

Any fire endurance model requires the following components:

1) Knowledge or predictive model of fire growth,
2) Knowledge or predictive model for heat transfer,
3) Degrade model for main wood components,
4) Degrade model for connections,
5) Structural analysis model capable of accommodating changes in properties over time.

Fire endurance modeling is a culmination of both thermal and mechanical modeling of the interactions that occur between structure and fire. The needed components of a fire endurance model for a wood assembly require information or models at some level of complexity from all the major areas of fire research. Many of the references cited above under thermal degrade research also contain a structural computation component. Fire endurance model development is truly an interdisciplinary problem and cannot rely on structural engineering expertise alone. Various levels of simplification are suitable in some cases and have been applied selectively in existing models. For example, some models are geared toward predicting fire endurance of members in a standard fire endurance test, simplifying the need for fire growth knowledge (Lie 1992). Some methods are intended for design (Janssens 1994) and others are research tools. Sullivan et al. (1994) and Hosser et al. (1994) provide reviews and comparisons of existing numerical methods devoted to structural analysis and design for fire conditions. Sometimes, prediction of the fire endurance of a single representative component such as a joist, stud or truss may be adequate for estimating the fire endurance of a multiple component floor or wall assembly. In cases where material properties, fire temperatures, or structure characteristics vary substantially across the assembly, the assembly and these variations must be considered directly in models to predict fire endurance (Cramer and White 1996).

Fire endurance models quickly become very complex as their sophistication and range of applicability increase. The input needs for these models can quickly out pace our knowledge of material performance and render a model highly dependent on the uncertainty in largely unknown material and thermal response. The challenge in fire endurance research will not only be the development of computational models that can operate on a designer's desktop computer, but the development of reliable and robust models for which input properties are generally available.

The Need for Coordinated Research Efforts

When one compares the current state of structural wood fire endurance knowledge with that of twenty years ago (Schaffer 1977), considerable progress has been achieved. Most of the progress has consisted of individual efforts undertaken more or less in parallel around the world. Certainly, more could have been achieved had these efforts been coordinated and such coordination will be needed in the future to accelerate the next level of advance in fire endurance research.

Approximately ten years ago, a group of researchers formed together to share fire modeling research in an organization called the North American Wood Products Fire Research Consortium (NAWPFRC). This group meets yearly with an open-door policy for anyone conducting wood fire endurance modeling research to share their findings. The wood fire research community is small and spread far across the world. The NAWPFRC yearly exchange of information has prevented research from being duplicated in North America. Major future advances in fire endurance research can most effectively be achieved, by not only a sharing of research, but a formal integration of different advances achieved internationally. Most research efforts are nationally based and funding sources tend to discourage international research projects. Yet such collaboration offers the greatest potential for advance. An organized, integration of heat transfer modeling efforts, thermal degrade research, and fire endurance research is needed to achieve the most powerful fire endurance models. The international wood fire research community should actively seek funding mechanisms that will promote such a cooperative effort.

Summary

The emergence of performance-based codes is demanding greater knowledge of structural fire performance and the development of means to compute fire endurance. Greater understanding of fire growth, heat transfer processes, material property changes, and assembly performance is needed to support the move toward performance-based codes and improved fire safety. The most likely advances will consist of computer-based models that can be used by designers and researchers. While advances in each individual area are needed, the integration of these advances is needed for greatest impact. The interdisciplinary nature of fire endurance research increases the need and potential benefit for formal, collaborative research efforts that cross international boundaries.

Acknowledgments

The helpful suggestions during preparation of this paper of John Kerns and James Shaw of Weyerhaeuser are gratefully acknowledged.

Appendix - References

Badger, S.G. (1996). 1995 large loss fires and explosions. *NFPA J.* Nov./Dec., 58-78.

Brannigan, F.L. (1988). Are wood trusses good for your health? *Fire Engineering.* June, 73-79.

Buchanan, A.H. and Barnett, J. (1995). Performance based design for fire in New Zealand. *Restructuring: America and Beyond, Proceedings of Structures Congress XIII.* 1995 April 2-5; Boston, MA. American Society of Civil Engineers, New York, NY., 1, 1106-1121

Buchanan, A.H. and Thomas, G.C. (1996). Predicting the real fire performance of light frame timber construction. *Proceedings, Wood and Fire Safety, 3rd International Scientific Conference*, 6-9 May 1996, The High Tatras, Slovak Republic. Zvolen: Technical University Zvolen, Faculty of Wood Technology, 21-30.

Bukowski, R.W. and Babrauskas, V. (1994). Developing rational, performance-based fire safety requirements in model building codes. *Fire and Materials*. 18(3): 173-191.

Clancy, P. (1996). Sensitivity study of variables affecting time-of-failure of wood framed walls in fire. *Proceedings of the International Wood Engineering Conference '96*, New Orleans, LA, Oct. 27-Nov. 1, 1996.Vol. 2, pg. 2-263 - 2-268.

Clancy, P., Beck, V.R. and Leicester, R.H. (1995). Time dependent probability of failure of wood frames in real fire. *Proceedings of the 4th International Fire and Materials Conference and Exhibition*. InterScience Communications Limited, London, England. 85-94.

Corbett, G.P. 1988. Lightweight wood truss floor construction: a fire lesson. *Fire Engineering*, 7: 41-43.

Cramer, S. M. and White, J., 1993. "Flux-time exposure - a fire endurance measure for lumber," *Proceedings of the 2nd International Fire and Materials Conference*, InterScience Communications Ltd., London, UK, Sept. 1993.

Cramer, S.M., and White R.H. 1996. Fire endurance model for wood structural systems, *Proceedings of the International Wood Engineering Conference '96*, New Orleans, LA, Oct. 27-Nov. 1, 1996.Vol. 2, pg. 2-249 - 2-256.

Grundahl, K. (1992). *National engineered lightweight construction fire research project- Technical report: Literature search and technical analysis*. National Fire Protection Research Foundation, Quincy, MA. 225 pp.

Hall, J.R. (1996). Whatever happened to combustion toxicity. *Fire Technology* 32(4), 351-371.

Hosser, D., Dorn, T., Richter, E. (1994). Evaluation of simplified calculation methods for structural fire design. *Fire Safety Journal*. 22, 249-304.

Imaizumi, C. (1962). Stability in fire of protected and unprotected glued laminated beams. *Norsk. Skogind*. 16(4), 140-151.

Itani, R.Y. And Faherty, K.F. (Editors) (1984). *Structural wood research: state-of-the-art and research needs:* Proceedings of the workshop held at the Marc Plaza Hotel, Milwaukee, Wisconsin, Oct. 5 and 6, 1983. American Society of Civil Engineers, New York. 210 pp.

Janssens, M. (1994). Fire resistance of exposed timber beams and columns. *Proceedings of the Third International Fire and Materials Conference.* InterScience Communications Limited, London, England, 31-40.

King, E.G. and Glowinski, R.W. (1988). A rationalized model for calculating the fire endurance of wood beams. *Forest Prod. J.* 38(10), 31-36.

Konig, J. (1994). Structural fire design of timber structures according to Eurocode 5, Part 1.2. *Proceedings of the Pacific Timber Engineering Conference.* Timber Research and Development Advisory Council, Queensland, Australia, Vol. 2, 539-548.

König, J. and Norén, J. (1995). Wood construction behavior in natural/parametric fires. *Proceedings of the 4th International Fire and Materials Conference and Exhibition.* InterScience Communications Limited, London, England, 95-104.

Krupa, J. (1996). Performance-based code in fire resistance: a first attempt by Eurocodes. Presented at the International Conference on Performance-Based Codes and Fire Safety Design Methods, Ottawa, Canada, Sept. 24-26.

Lau, P. And Barrett, D. (1997). Modelling tension strength behavior of structural lumber exposed to elevated temperatures. Proceedings, 5th International Symposium on Fire safety Science, March 2-7, Melbourne, Victoria, Australia.

Lie, T.T. (1977). A method for assessing the fire resistance of laminated timber beams and columns. *Can. J. of Civil Eng.* 4, 161-169.

Lie, T.T. (Editor) (1992). *Structural fire protection.* ASCE Manuals and Reports on Engineering Practice No. 78. American Society of Civil Engineers, New York, NY. 241 pp.

Malanga, R. (1995). Fire endurance of lightweight wood trusses in building construction. *Fire Technology,* 31(1): 44-61 National Fire Protection Association, Quincy, MA

Mehaffey, J.R., Cuerrier, P. and Carisse, G. (1994). Model for heat transfer through gypsum-board/wood-stud walls exposed to fire. *Fire and Materials* 18(5), 297-305.

Norén, J.B. (1988). Failure of structural timber when exposed to fire. *Proceedings of the 1988 International Conference on Timber Engineering.* Vol. 2. Forest Products Society, Madison, WI., 397-401.

Norén, J. (1996). Load-bearing capacity of nailed joints exposed to fire. *Fire and Materials,* Vol. 20, 133-143.

Puchovsky, M. (1996). NFPA's perspectives on performance-based codes and standards.

Fire Technology. 32(4), 323-332.

Richardson, L.R. and McPhee, R.A. (1996). Fire-resistance and sound-transmission-class ratings for wood-frame walls. *Fire and Materials*. 20, 123-131.

Schaffer, E.L. (1973). Effect of pyrolytic temperature on the longitudinal strength of dry Douglas-fir. *J. of Testing and Eval.*, 1(4), 319-329.

Schaffer, E.L. (1977). State of structural timber fire endurance. *Wood and Fiber*, 9(2): 145-170.

Schaffer, E.L. (1982). Chapter 3. Influence of heat on the longitudinal creep of dry Douglas-fir. *Proceedings on Structural Use of Wood in Adverse Environments*. Meyer, R.W. and Kellogg, R.M., eds. Van Nostrand Reinhold Co., New York., 20-52.

Schaffer, E.L. (1988). How well do wood trusses really perform during a fire? *Fire J.* March/April:57-63.

Shrestha, D., Cramer, S. and White, R. (1995). Simplified Models for the Properties of Dimension Lumber and Metal-Plate Connections at Elevated Temperatures. *Forest Prod. J.*, 45(7/8):35-42.

SFPE (Society of Fire Protection Engineers) (1995). SFPE handbook of fire protection engineering. 2nd Ed. National Fire Protection Assoc., Quincy, MA.

Sullivan, P.J.E., Terro, M.J. and Morris, W.A. (1994). Critical review of fire-dedicated thermal and structural computer programs. *J. Applied Fire Science*. 3(2), 113-135.

Tanaka, T. (1994). Concept and framework of a performance based fire safety design for buildings. *J. of Applied Fire Science*. 3(4):335-358

Takeda, H. And Mehaffey, J.R. (1996). Model for predicting fire resistance performance of wood-stud walls with or without insulation. *Proceedings of the International Wood Engineering Conference '96*, New Orleans, LA, Oct. 27-Nov. 1, 1996.Vol. 2, 2-257 - 2-262.

The World Almanac and Book of Facts 1997. (1997). Famighetti, R. Editor. K-III Reference Corporation, Mahwah, New Jersey.

White, R.H. (1984). Use of coatings to improve fire resistance of wood. *Standard Technical Publication 826*. American Society for Testing and Materials.

White, R.H. (1995). Analytical methods for determining fire resistance of timber members, *Chpt. 11. The SFPE Handbook of Fire Protection Engineering*. 2nd Ed. Society of Fire Protection Engineers: 4-217-4-229.

White, R.H. and Nordheim, E.V. (1992).   Charring rate of wood for ASTM E 119 exposure. *Fire Technology*. 28(1),5-30.

White, R.H. and Tran, H. (1996). Charring rate of wood exposed to a constant flux. *Proceedings, Wood and Fire Safety*, 3rd International Scientific Conference, 6-9 May 1996, The High Tatras, Slovak Republic. Zvolen: Technical University Zvolen, Faculty of Wood Technology, 175-183.

Zeller, E.J. (1997).   Standards in codes - a building official's perspective.   *ASTM Standardization News*, January, 30-32.

Evaluation, Preservation and Rehabilitation

Edward F. Diekmann[1], Member ASCE

Abstract

The continued use or reuse of older buildings utilizing wood elements pose many challenges to the practicing engineer and offer many opportunities for productive and useful research. This paper presents some of these challenges and opportunities from the viewpoint of a practicing engineer.

Introduction

An engineer in the course of his practice may confront a variety of structures with wooden components of a variety of ages. Broadly speaking these structures can be separated into residential structures constructed with what today is referred to as "light framing," commercial/industrial heavy timber structures utilizing post and beam framing, and "engineered" structures such as a timber bridge. Commercial/industrial structures frequently have engineered components in the form of roof trusses. The timber frame with mortise and tenon joints assembled with wooden pegs, as found most commonly in early barns, is a specialized type of structure much less likely to be encountered.

Evaluation

Evaluation usually starts with a walk-through inspection. Absent obvious decay and/or sagging and clearly distressed members, the initial inspection usually provides little direct assistance beyond its value in helping to define the scope of work. A serious evaluation requires dimensioned plans which, for structures more than about

---

[1] Consulting Structural Engineer
44 Kingston Road, Kensington, CA 94707

30 years old, are usually non-existent. Plans usually have to be created and there is no way to accomplish this short of photos with field measurements and the subsequent creation in the office of as-built plans. It is axiomatic that the first visit to obtain measurements will miss at least one important measurement so that at least one additional visit will be required. Follow-up visits will almost certainly be needed as the evaluation becomes more detailed and information regarding actual member dimensions, bolt sizes, end distances, bearing area for beams and similar data assumes importance. The completed plans should show the structural support and bracing system in sufficient detail to be the basis for the analytical evaluation that will follow.

Evaluation, as with design, should concern itself with both the structure's capabilities to support vertical loads and to resist lateral loads. Most wood-frame structures employ post and beam construction utilizing simple spans and do not represent a challenge to analyze for vertical load. Some portions of these structures, particularly residential light-frame roofs, may not have a well-defined structural system and instead seem to rely on some indeterminate interaction of beam and plate action not amenable to analysis. Does an engineer introduce members into such a roof which has functioned for perhaps 70 years merely to provide a system which he can understand and analyze? This is perhaps more of a concern if such a structure is to be modified because of uncertainty as to whether the modifications may affect some element critical to its past behavior. This very uncertainty may justify additions to bring about a determinant system.

Most older structures were not provided with a designed lateral bracing system, but were rather constructed utilizing materials and details which experience indicated would result in a structure giving satisfactory performance. The continued existence of these structures shows that these judgments were generally correct. An engineer can only feel foolish adding designed wind bracing into a 100 year old building, unless the addition is to accommodate extreme wind loadings. The situation is somewhat different with seismic bracing because the structure may not yet have experienced "the big one." Even if it has experienced a large or great quake, there is reason to suspect that the next "big one" may produce a different ground motion and potentially a different result on the structure. The structure may also have deteriorated since the previous event. Recent cyclical testing has produced nail fatigue failure which suggests the previous "big one," even without causing significant observed structural damage, may have opened a doorway to failure by reducing the remaining number of load cycles before loss of the nails. Considerably more testing must be done before any conclusion can be drawn that compensatory strengthening might be needed on wood bracing systems which have experienced "the big one."

The evaluation process will eventually produce design stresses in the members and the first serious problem for the engineer. What are the allowable stresses on the various members? The engineer can specify a species and grade of timber for a new design and this selection will have a set of assigned allowable stresses, but in an existing structure, possibly one build before lumber was graded, no such stresses are available. The only presently available answer is to send out a grader to grade the material. This is not a complete answer, however, because the grader cannot usually see all four sides and an end as required for complete visual grading. Can techniques be developed or refined for evaluating timber in situ and assigning allowable stresses?

There are large numbers of structures which were engineered to the standards of their day, but which are over-stressed by the newer standards of today. Typical of the problem are truss tension chords designed for an allowable tension stress equal to the allowable bending stress when today's practice allows a tension stress of only 55 percent of the allowable bending stress. These members are "over-stressed" by about 80 percent, even if originally otherwise properly designed. Similar design "over-stresses" have been produced by the assignment of new design stresses for deeper dimension lumber resulting from the in-grade test program. For example, every sawn lumber purlin in every panelized roof built prior to the new design stresses is now "over-stressed" by about 50 percent due to the new and lower allowable stresses assigned to such members. There was a period of time when glulam beams were available with a 2600 psi bending stress, a value subsequently recognized as too high and abandoned. Does it automatically follow from the presence of these "over-stresses" that the member or connection must be reinforced?

In historic times the capacity of a bolt or connector joint was governed solely by the number of fasteners in the joint and the provision of sufficient cross sectional area of timber at the critical section. This frequently resulted in large numbers of fasteners in each row. Current design practice reduces the efficiency of fasteners in a row starting with three, the reduction becoming increasingly large as the number of fasteners in a row increases. Virtually every old bolt or connector joint is over-stressed, many very seriously, as a result of this change in design practice. The efficiency adjustments are based on elastic behavior applicable to other materials as well and theory and tests indicate that the fasteners in a multi-fastener row are not equally loaded as early design practice assumed but rather are unequally loaded with the first and last fasteners in the row getting most of the load. This behavior is true in steel connections, but it is assumed because steel yields and is ductile that at ultimate load the load per fastener will be equal because of yielding of the initially more heavily loaded fasteners and steel connections are typically designed without efficiency adjustments. Why should connections in wood dependent on an interplay between a ductile steel element and crushing wood be adjusted for elastic efficiency? More pertinently, are connections designed without efficiency adjustments sufficiently over-stressed that they must be reinforced?

Evaluation of older structures is made more complicated by the fact that wood is subject to a duration of load effect, i.e., wood fatigues. The time to failure is related to the ratio of the level of stress to the failure stress, the closer the stress level under load is to the expected failure stress level of the piece the shorter the time to actual failure. The load duration effect is currently defined by the so-called Madison curve, developed from bending stress data with significant scatter, but applied to wood regardless of the nature of the induced stress. The same factors are also applied to connections in wood. Research indicates the duration of load effect varies with the type of stress in the wood and also indicates certain types of connections cause stress increases in the adjacent wood, both indications that the "Madison curve" is not necessarily reliable in evaluating specific members and connections. Some research results have been interpreted as indicating that the duration of load effect also vary with the grade of lumber, the interruption or distortion of the grain caused by knots causing stress riser effects which in short time tests cause mechanical failure before a duration of load effect is observable and which in the longer term would still be operating to shorten the time to failure by increasing the ratio of induced stress to the failure stress. Should duration of load adjustments be altered, particularly where changes in assigned stresses or in design practice give rise to "over-stresses"?

Assignment of stresses to wood members and adjustments for duration of load are based on statistical analysis of group behavior, i.e., a given "grade." The evaluator is confronted with a need to know the ultimate strength of a specific piece or pieces. The assignment of a piece to a given structural grade is controlled primarily by the presence of the largest knot or knot cluster and the greatest slope of grain and these grade-controlling defects are not necessarily in the critically stressed portions of the member. Accurate evaluation may require a careful field determination of defect location, in effect a section-by-section grade determination. Can a convenient method be devised to scan a member in situ and assign a strength section-by-section? Ignoring defects, i.e., assuming clear material, what is needed to predict breaking strength and how accurately can this be done for a specific member?

The evaluation processes discussed have implied lumber that is physically intact. Unfortunately many structures have not remained intact, but have been exposed to moisture with resultant decay or to termites, both phenomenon which remove sound wood from the member. The extent of this removal or even its existence may not be apparent. While advanced decay, so called "dry rot," is usually readily apparent, the extent to which the fungus has weakened the wood where decay is just commencing or where this attack extends beyond the obviously decayed area, is not apparent. Large beams subjected to small amounts of water on the top can decay from the top down and the inside out with the decay entirely hidden from view by an outer shall of wood with a moisture content too low to support decay fungus. First-hand experience shows that this can occur without visible water stains on the ceiling or adjacent framing and it should not be assumed that because there are no outward signs of decay where there is even a hint of water exposure, no decay exists. Termite damage is almost never apparent until the wood is largely destroyed. Can a scanning method developed for intact members be applied to damaged members?

Large sawn timbers frequently develop checks due to the stresses induced by drying shrinkage. These checks often pass through the connections intersecting the axis of bolts or passing across shear plates or splint rings installed in the surface of the piece. What is the effect of such splits on the connection capacity?

Wood frame structures are most frequently braced by shearwalls. In older structures these walls were not designed, but are rather the solid sheathed walls provided to enclose the building or provide separation of the various interior functions. Very little hard data is available on the bracing capabilities of these historic materials. What information may be available has not been well or widely disseminated. What are reasonable shear design values to assign to these materials?

The engineer in making a lateral analysis of a light -frame structure frequently ignores much of the building. For example, in a building with lath and plaster walls and ceilings, the integration of the ceiling lath and plaster on the underside of a floor with the wall lath and plaster is ignored as a potential load path for lateral load from the floor and only the connection of the floor joists and/or blocking to the wall plate, i.e., the rough framing, is analyzed. This situation results from the lack of knowledge about the load transfer capabilities of finishes and constructions of this sort.

The problems of proper lateral analysis of light-frame structures go well beyond the simple issue just discussed. Accurate analysis of such a structure for the lateral load induced by the wind or an earthquake is almost certainly beyond our current engineering capabilities. Some of these difficulties in doing an accurate analysis were recently presented by Diekmann. The purpose here is not to delve into these difficulties, but to note that uncertainties about the accuracy of the available analytical methods increases the difficulties in determining whether failures in the overall structural bracing system to provide the capacity the calculations indicate is required denotes a deficiency that needs to be corrected. This problem exists in new structures which can meet building code prescriptive bracing requirements and which at the same time fail to provide the capacity required by an engineering analysis. At what point of calculated short-fall in bracing capacity must strengthening occur?

For undamaged members and structures, the problems found during the evaluation normally take the form of a non-compliance with some aspect of building code requirements. The computed design stress, for example, exceeds the current allowable stress. If it is an over-stress, how much over-stress is required to trigger a repair? Five percent? Ten? Twenty? Is 50 percent, which defines a dangerous building under the Dangerous Building Code, an acceptable level? Sometimes the problem takes the form of a violation of an arbitrary rule. For example, the end distance is violated on the last bolt in a multi-bolt tension connection or one of the most hotly discussed problems in California, the nails in the plywood of a plywood shearwall are over-driven. What is the proper value to ascribe to the non-compliant assembly? It is a comparatively easy task to determine that a code provision has been violated, it is quite another to decide if the violation has given rise to a condition that must be addressed. Typically the basis for the design rule is not available and the consequences of the violation are not spelled out, the rule reflects the research and the violating condition was not researched. It is such conundrums that test the engineer's judgment.

<u>Preservation</u>

The preservation of timber structures is very simply in concept; keep them dry and free of wood-destroying pests. This is relatively easy to accomplish when dealing with members in enclosed space. It is difficult-to-impossible to accomplish on structures where the wood elements have been deliberately exposed to the weather as part of the architectural appearance and the introduction of weather protection in the form of some sort of skin on or over the members would radically alter the architectural appearance. Even where such a skin is accepted, great care is required in its application because any penetration of water under the skin may accelerate the very decay process the skin was intended to prevent.

A moisture content in the wood of about 20 percent is required to support decay. The moisture content of a piece of wood, absent active water, is dependent on the relative humidity of the atmosphere surrounding the piece. Control of this atmosphere through adequate ventilation, temperature regulation, and control of introduced moisture is a necessity if decay is to be avoided. Unheated spaces with wooden floors over unventilated crawlspace areas and high humidity atmospheres such as those at indoor swimming pools, laundries and certain cooking and industrial processes pose particular risks and need to have improved ventilation and/or humidity controls provided to forestall the advance of the decay found in the evaluation process.

<u>Rehabilitation</u>

Presumably the evaluation has identified the problems with individual members and/or the structures as a whole followed by a decision as to what problems must be addressed. An initial question that must be answered in addressing these problems is: Are the current looks important? If the answer is "no," then the full range of potential solutions is available; finishes may be removed to add shearwalls, new beams and posts may be added, additional pieces may be scabbed onto over-stressed members, sections of structure may be demolished and rebuilt. In short, all possibilities may be explored and the final solution picked solely on the basis of economics.

A "yes" answer immediately restricts the available options and raises potentially severe cost considerations. The restoration community has great talents and can replicate virtually any construction and appearance. It is thus conceivable that the element that needs rehabilitation could be removed, the needed repair or strengthening done, the element replaced or rebuilt, and the work finished to look as it looked originally. This can be very expensive and may run afoul of the preservationists who will object to the fact that the rehabilitated element is not "original" and thus unacceptable even if visually indistinguishable from the original.

An over-stressed but undamaged member may be strengthened in a variety of ways. It may be replaced with a similar sized member having better structural properties. Replacement, however, necessitates support of the load being carried by the original member while the replacement is being accomplished with its attendant cost and difficulties. In some cases major removal and replacement of other building components may be necessary to clear a path for removing and replacing the over-stressed member. In some cases physical impediments in the building may make removal and replacement virtually impossible.

The easiest method for strengthening an over-stressed member is to add additional material. The added material may be wood or steel and the material may be added to either share the load or to work compositely with the original member. A steel channel or an added wood beam bolted to the side of an existing beam are examples of a load-sharing strengthening while a steel plate lag screwed to the bottom of a beam would represent a composite strengthening. Experience indicates that engineers who have no problem accepting the concept of composite behavior between steel and concrete have a problem accepting the same principles when applied to wood and steel. A decision must be made when adding material as to whether or not the existing element is to be partially or completely relieved of the existing stresses. Such relief requires some type of sharing with its related costs. If the over-stresses are largely induced by code imposed live loads, it may be feasible to leave the existing member carrying the dead load stresses and the combined or composite element to share the live load stresses, eliminating the need of any sharing. This approach is not available if the dead load stress is already near the allowable stress on the member.

Composite testing

An option exists for reinforcing beams and the tension chords of trusses in the form of post-tensioning. The engineering community is generally unaware that post-tensioning of wood members is completely feasible and reliable and has a considerable history of successful application. The stressing can be done with either rods or strands, although strands are typically used. This method is particularly useful where access is difficult - it is much easier to string one or two cables than to handle and position a long rigid member to be scabbed on — and it is particularly appropriate with trusses where connections for the strands can usually be made to the steel in the heel joints, by-passing completely questions about the adequacy of the multi-bolt connections usually found at these locations. The ability to set the level of the force applied is also very useful, as is the fact that the application of an active force can offset historic deflection or sag. The strands must be added externally which can be an appearance problem and on occasion a fire consideration. The big problem with this method involves the connection of the anchorage for the strands to the wood. The tensioning forces are usually sufficiently large that a heavy attachment is necessary that is difficult to fit to the available wood. Some proprietary work has been done in the United States to investigate anchorages using dowels in epoxy-filled holes followed by successful application in the field. Extensive work has been done in other countries to develop connections in wood using rods and epoxies and this work should be imported, expanded if necessary, and then imparted to the engineering community.

A damaged member, over-stressed or not, can pose an additional problem. Total replacement is an obvious possibility. The addition of scabbed-on members to take some or all of the load is also feasible. It may be desirable to remove the damage, the rot or termite destruction, and replace the lost material. How is the replaced material to be effectively integrated with the material that remains? There appears to have been substantial research done suggesting that steel plates or rods can be epoxied to sound wood to transfer bending forces or stresses and that missing wood itself can be replaced by epoxies. Much of this work has been proprietary, at least some of it may not be reliable from a structural point of view, and most of it remains unknown to the general engineering community. The basic question is: How good and how reliable are such repairs? A state-of-the-art report on what is known on member repair with epoxies would be most valuable.

A standard method of increasing the bracing in a wood structure, other than the addition of shearwalls, is through the addition of steel rigid frames. There should be serious concerns about this approach because of questions about the relative rigidities of the frames and any shearwalls. Not only is quality data lacking with which to determine the rigidity of shearwalls, but the rigidity of the diaphragm which is delivering loads to the shearwalls is also uncertain. In many cases no alternative to the steel frames is available and frames must be added, but the frame rigidity could be adjusted for compatibility with the rest of the bracing if only the rigidity of the other components could be accurately determined. The tributary area approach, the most widely used method for allocating loads to bracing elements in wood structures, must be in error, but is the error of such a magnitude as to be a concern? If the answer is "no," then the rigidity of the various bracing elements is irrelevant.

Conclusion

The evaluation, preservation and rehabilitation of wood buildings pose many challenges to the engineer. A few of these have been covered in the preceding discussion. A summary of some of the questions waiting for answers is as follows:

- How are allowable stresses to be determined for in site members?
- What is an allowable over-stress for a wood member? A connection in wood? Can levels of risk be set for levels of over-stresses?
- What are the capacities of older, multi-bolt connections?
- Should duration of load factors be changed (or new ones developed) for over-stressed members or connections?
- Can techniques be developed to assess section loss due to decay or termite damage?
- What are the shear racking strengths of various historic materials?
- What would has been done or should be done to verify that wood works compositely with other materials?
- What is the state-of-the-art in wood, epoxy joints and reinforcement?
- How can shearwall and diaphragm rigidities be accurately assessed?
- How can wood structures be more accurately analyzed for lateral loads?

Appendix 1

References

Diekmann, Edward F (1995) "Design and Code Issues in the Design of Diaphragms and Shearwalls," Proceedings Earthquake Performance and Safety of Timber Structures, Annual meeting of Forest Products Society, Madison, WI

WOOD IN INFRASTRUCTURE:
ANALYSIS OF RESEARCH NEEDS AND GOALS

Russell C. Moody and Michael A. Ritter[1]

Abstract

Two related government initiatives, the Intermodal Surface Transportation Efficiency Act and the Wood in Transportation Program, have resulted in significant activity in research and technology transfer for using wood for transportation structures. This paper reviews accomplishments and activities and suggests research needs for wood transportation structures. It also describes research needs for related structures such as waterfront and utility applications.

INTRODUCTION

Prior to the 20th century, most transportation structures in North America were made of wood. During this century, concrete and steel have replaced wood in many applications. Advances in alternate materials have played a major role in these changes. For example, timber bridges amount to about 10% of the total bridges in the United States, and another significant percentage of bridges have timber decks. Many of these structures containing wood are old and have exceeded their design life.

Although wood has been recognized by some as a viable material for short-span bridges, prior to 1988 little emphasis was placed on improving the structural and economic efficiency of bridges and other wood transportation structures. Recognizing the potential for wood to meet some needs for revitalizing the transportation infrastructure, Congress passed the Timber Bridge Initiative in 1988. This was followed by the 1991 Intermodal Surface Transportation Efficiency Act (ISTEA). Both of these national programs included provisions for research, demonstration, and technology transfer. The Timber Bridge Initiative, which has become the Wood in Transportation Program, is the responsibility of the U.S. Department of Agriculture, Forest Service (Cesa and Russell 1996); ISTEA is the responsibility of the U.S. Department of Transportation, Federal Highway Administration (FHWA) (Duwadi and Wood 1996).

---

[1] U.S. Department of Agriculture, Forest Service, Forest Products Laboratory, One Gifford Pinchot Drive, Madison, WI 53705–2398. The Forest Products Laboratory is maintained in cooperation with the University of Wisconsin. This article was written and prepared by U.S. Government employees on official time, and it is therefore in the public domain and not subject to copyright.

The Forest Service and the FHWA formed a joint research program to address needs for improved wood utilization in transportation structures (Wipf et al. 1993). Activities in the United States have renewed international interest in the use of wood bridges. Cooperative research programs with several countries were described at the 1996 International Wood Engineering Conference (Gopu 1996). Results of U.S. research between 1988 and 1996 have been periodically reported (Duwadi and Ritter 1995, Ritter and Moody 1991, Ritter et al. 1994,1996e) and were summarized at a recent conference co-sponsored by the Forest Products Laboratory of the USDA Forest Service and the FHWA; international activities are also described in the proceedings (Ritter et al. 1996a).

These two major initiatives have focused on highway structures, recognizing that many results could apply to other transportation structures as well as other exterior uses. The objective of this paper is to provide a general assessment of the present state of knowledge and research needs as they apply to all types of transportation structures and other related structures such as waterfront and utility applications. Basic references included (1) the assessment of research needs in 1983 (Gutkowski and Williamson 1984), (2) results of the initial research needs assessment (Wipf et al. 1993), (3) results of a 1994 workshop on research needs for engineered wood products for transportation structures (Dickson 1996), and (4) proceedings of the 1996 National Conference on Wood Transportation Structures (Ritter et al. 1996a).

The scope of this report includes structures for highways, railroads, utilities, and waterfronts. The report also addresses material property research needs that apply to structures for many uses. It does not include a thorough analysis nor ranking of these needs. More detailed analysis is needed with input from a broad user-based audience.

HIGHWAY STRUCTURES

Bridges

General—Significant advances have been made in developing design criteria for the stress-laminated deck system (Crews et al. 1994). Results of extensive field evaluation of stress-laminated decks after several years service are being reported (Hislop and Ritter 1996, Kainz et al. 1996b, Lee et al. 1996b, Ritter et al. 1996b,1996d, Wacker et al. 1996, Wacker and Ritter 1992,1995a,1995b), and design procedures and construction practices have been recommended (Ritter et al. 1995c, Ritter and Lee 1996e). The field evaluations demonstrate that a variety of wood materials can be used for this type of bridge (Hernandez et al. 1996, Kainz and Hill 1996a, Lee et al. 1996a, Manbeck et al. 1996a, Ritter et al. 1995b,1996c, Taylor and Ritter 1996). Innovative approaches are still being evaluated. For example, experimental bridges have been built using metal plate-connected trusses similar to those used for residential roof systems (Dagher et al. 1996a, Triche and Ritter 1996). Several types of T-beam and box systems have been utilized: one type uses a stress-laminated deck (Apple and Woodward 1996, Crews and Bakoss 1996, Dickson and GangaRao 1990) and another, components that are fully glued (Ritter et al. 1996c, Taylor and Ritter 1996). Detailed technical reports are being prepared for these various systems that should form the basis for determining whether and what additional research is needed.

Load distribution—The assumed distribution of vehicle loads on highway bridges is a key element of design that can significantly affect size, cost, and performance. Thus, accurate load distribution criteria are critical to structural efficiency and economics. Field evaluations of various types of bridges that include load tests are providing valuable information on load distribution. These data need to be compared with present design criteria to determine if design efficiencies can be improved. Research is needed on options for improving load distribution in systems such as plank decks and structural glued laminated timber (glulam) panel decks.

Dynamic performance—Current design criteria for timber bridges do not require an increase in loading to account for the dynamic effect of moving vehicles, as is required for other materials. Recently, this practice has been questioned and some design engineers believe that a dynamic factor is applicable to timber bridges. Questions about the performance of bridges under dynamic and impact loading are being addressed through analysis of full-scale test results (Wipf et al. 1996), which will result in more accurate design criteria related to the performance of timber bridges under dynamic loading.

Rail systems—Many bridges built today must be provided with crash-tested railings. Although numerous railings have been crash tested for steel and concrete bridges, relatively few have been developed for timber bridges. Full-scale crash testing of rail systems for a number of timber bridges with longitudinal decks has resulted in FHWA acceptance (Faller et al. 1996). Detailed drawings are available for the rail types commonly required for longitudinal timber decks on secondary road systems (Ritter et al. 1995a). Rail systems have also been developed and have met criteria for low-volume roads (Faller et al. 1995). Two rails for transverse timber decks have been investigated, but results have not yet been published. Research is needed on additional options for using transverse decks on secondary roads.

Capacity assessment—Guidelines are being developed for using stress-wave technology to determine in-place capacity of bridge components (Pellerin et al. 1996). Similar techniques have been shown to be applicable for timber piling, which supports many bridge abutments (Anthony and Pandey 1996), and for measuring the stiffness of bridge decks (Ross et al. 1996). Additional research underway is examining alternate techniques. Many composite concrete–wood bridges systems have been built, and methods are needed to determine their in-place capacity.

Maintenance/rehabilitation—There is a significant inventory of short-span timber bridges that continue to meet the needs of many highways. Economical methods are needed for maintaining and rehabilitating these bridges. Virtually no research has been devoted to this subject during the past several years, and the state-of-the-art remains as described by Ritter (1990).

Sound Barriers

Wood products have been popular choices for sound barriers along highways in urban areas. However, some materials and designs have resulted in serviceability problems. Research is underway to determine successful combinations of materials and designs that meet desired performance and aesthetic requirements (Boothby et al. 1996). Additional research should be based on the results of that study. Some material options to consider would be the possible advantages of wood–nonwood composites, possibly including recycled materials, as well as improved structural panels. This general area is addressed in the section on Material Properties.

Sign and Rail Posts

Information on performance is needed to improve acceptance criteria. Alternative or improved wood–nonwood composites may offer advantages for the performance of sign and rail posts upon impact. Another potential research area is techniques for improving the durability of the posts.

Retaining Walls

Retaining walls is another area where wood–nonwood composites and recycled materials may offer some advantages. Standardized designs would enhance use and acceptance of both wood and wood–nonwood composites.

Other Areas for Research

Portable crossings—The changing approach to forest operations such as harvesting will likely result in less permanent roads and bridges. Portable bridges are proving to be an economical and environmentally sound solution for crossing streams and unstable areas (Hislop 1996, Taylor et al. 1996, Taylor and Ritter 1996). Improved and standardized designs could enhance their acceptance.

Pedestrian bridges—Timber is a popular material for pedestrian bridges because of both economics and aesthetics. Several demonstration bridges have been built as part of the Forest Service program, but there has been no formal research effort in this area. An effort is need to develop several standardized design approaches.

RAILWAY STRUCTURES

Throughout most of the 20th century, wood has been used for railroad ties, and timber structures have been extensively used by the railroads for crossing streams, lowlands, and highways. Countless miles of timber trestle bridges continue to carry increasing tonnage each year. Railway engineers are facing a challenge in dealing with an aging inventory of structures, many of which are more than 50 years old, while being asked to upgrade the structures to carry heavier loads. Many of these structures consist of heavy timbers in sizes that are no longer readily available. Thus, replacement is a major challenge, in addition to upgrading.

Bridges

Some new systems being investigated for highway bridges provide for better load distribution. Using these systems to rehabilitate or replace railway bridges could increase their capacity. Also, improved grading methods for existing timbers that result in increased design properties could enhance upgrading of structures (see Material Properties). Dynamic loading is also a concern on railway bridges (see Highway Structures). Efforts are also needed to include the latest design criteria adopted for wood highway bridges and wood buildings in railroad specifications.

Ties

Improving the performance of railroad ties is particularly challenging because of the relatively low cost of existing ties, most of which have a long service-life. Most problems develop in the connections between the rail, tie plate, and tie. The primary failure mechanism is in either compression perpendicular-to-grain, splitting, or spike withdrawal. Compression perpendicular-to-grain could be improved by modifying surface properties by laminating or using a wood–nonwood composite. Fastener performance can be improved through redesign of the fastener or modification of the fastened area, by laminating or using a wood–nonwood composite. The challenge will be to obtain improvements and maintain needed bending strength in a cost-effective manner compared to sawn treated timber ties. Extending service life will become more important as disposal of used ties becomes more difficult.

UTILITY STRUCTURES

Wood poles and crossarms represent the major support structures that have carried electricity, phone service, and cable TV service to our homes and businesses. With the types of changes that are occurring in these areas, it would be easy to predict the demise of the present infrastructure of poles and lines. For example, underground cables, wireless phones, and satellite dishes have the potential for replacing the old infrastructure and likely will in some areas. However, overhead lines continue to be the most economical method for transmitting and distributing electric power. Thus, power transmission and distribution systems are likely to continue to require poles and crossarms to support the lines.

Wood poles have always had a competitive advantage for distribution systems and some designs have been used for transmission structures. However, alternative materials are becoming more competitive. Improvements could improve the efficient use of wood in these applications (see Material Properties). Values applicable for design of many pole species, glulam timber, and Douglas-fir crossarms are presently given in ANSI standards (ANSI 1992,1995, 1996). There is a continuing need to ensure that these values are applicable to the changing resource. Research is need to establish values for design of other species for crossarms, notably Southern Pine. Maintenance of the existing inventory of wood poles is a high priority with many utilities. Technology for estimating the in-place capacity of existing poles is available (Anthony et al. 1992). Repair and strengthening techniques are needed.

WATERFRONT STRUCTURES

Our waterfront structures have historically been made using wood, most of it heavily treated with preservatives using a pressure process. In salt water environments, this treated wood has resisted both decay and marine borers. However, as a result of progress in improving the environmental quality of waterfront areas, two new problems have arisen: leaching of some preservative may not be acceptable, and the cleaner water has permitted the reintroduction of some types of marine borers that attack treated wood. Thus, new developments in either materials or protection are needed to meet the needs of waterfront structures (see Material Properties).

MATERIAL PROPERTIES

A wide variety of species and grades of wood can be used for bridges and other transportation structures. New grading procedures for hardwood lumber and for hardwood and softwood timbers provide for more efficient use of the resource (Green and McDonald 1993, Green et al. 1994,1996, McDonald et al. 1993,1996). Field trials are needed to demonstrate the advantages of improved grading to producers and users. Research has demonstrated that several hardwoods can be used to manufacture glulam having design properties comparable to those for Douglas-fir and Southern Pine, species widely used for glulam (Manbeck et al. 1993,1996,1996c, Moody et al. 1993).

For some transportation applications, particularly short-span bridges, shear strength controls the size of members. Research on the shear strength of glulam timber and sawn lumber has provided a better understanding of the variables affecting this strength property (Soltis and Rammer 1994, Rammer 1996, Rammer and Soltis 1994, Rammer and McLean 1996a,1996b, Rammer et al. 1996). Additional research is underway to better understand shear strength under slowly applied (static) loads. Research is needed to determine applicable shear design properties for use under the cyclic loading environment of many transportation structures. Research is also needed on applicable design properties in bending and shear for structural composite lumber products under the loading and environment of transportation structures.

The combination of wood with new synthetic fibers can greatly increase the bending strength of wood beams and potentially reduce the cost of major load-carrying members. Tingley et al. (1996) described a bridge constructed with fiber-reinforced plastic as a reinforcement for glulam. Development of that particular product is described in other references (Tingley 1990, Tingley and Cegelka 1996). Other research using various synthetic materials has also been described (Dagher et al. 1996b, Davalos et al. 1994, Galloway et al. 1996, Sonti et al. 1995). Research is needed to confirm the long-term satisfactory field performance of these new products.

Using recycled wood and fiber products in transportation structures would help alleviate predicted fiber shortages and provide an outlet for discarded preservative-treated material. Reuse of materials should be given priority; methods are needed to predict residual capacity. Combining wood in some form (strands, flakes, fibers) with other materials can provide a product with unique properties. Of particular importance in some transportation structures may be energy-absorption capability, such as demonstrated by a wood–cement composite (Wolfe and Gjinolli 1996). Wood–plastic composites have creep characteristics that may prohibit their use in applications with relatively high constant stress; however, their energy-absorption capability may be advantageous for rail posts.

For nearly all transportation structures, preservative treatment is necessary for long-term serviceability. Research has addressed treatability and durability of heartwood of some softwood species (Wang and DeGroot 1996) and several eastern hardwoods (Blankenhorn et al. 1996) used in demonstration bridges. Studies are also underway on new types of preservatives (Crawford and DeGroot 1996, DeGroot et al. 1996, Laks et al. 1996). Research is needed to accurately assess the environmental impacts of various types of preservative-treated wood.

TECHNOLOGY TRANSFER NEEDS

A high priority need has been standard plans for highway bridges. Standard plans have been prepared for several types of Southern Pine bridge deck systems (Lee et al. 1995), hardwood glulam bridges (Manbeck et al. 1996b), and crash-tested rail systems for longitudinal deck bridges (Ritter et al. 1995a). Standard plans are being prepared for bridge system superstructures (Lee and Wacker 1996c). Similar information is needed for bridge substructures, pedestrian bridges, and portable bridges. An interactive computer program is being prepared for analysis, design, rating, and drafting of highway bridge superstructures (Thomas and Puckett 1996). Additional efforts in this area should build on the information being developed.

Transferring technology for railway, waterfront, and utility applications presents unique challenges. Initially, priority will be given to participation on technical committees that prepare design standards for these uses. To effectively transfer existing and developing information, an Internet system is planned to link Forest Service and FHWA sites with many of the cooperators involved in the research program. Similar sites involving industry, universities, and other government agencies would be beneficial.

REFERENCES

ANSI. (1992). "Wood poles—specifications and dimensions." *ANSI O5.1*, American National Standards Institute, New York.

ANSI. (1995). "Solid sawn wood crossarms and braces—specifications and dimensions." *ANSI O5.3*, American National Standards Institute, New York.

ANSI. (1996). "Structural glued laminated timber for utility structures." *ANSI O5.2*, American National Standards Institute, New York.

Anthony, R. W., Bodig, J., Phillips, G. E., and Brooks, R. T. (1992). "Longitudinal NDE of new wood utility poles." *Rep. TR-100864*, Electric Power Research Institute, Palo Alto, Calif.

Anthony, R. W., and Pandey, A. K. (1996). "Determining the length of timber piles in transportation structures." *Proc., 1996 Natl. Conf. Wood Transportation Structures, FPL-GTR-94*, USDA Forest Service, Forest Products Laboratory, Madison, Wis., 427–436.

Apple, D. A., and Woodward, C. (1996). "Stress-laminated/steel T-beam bridge system." *Proc., 1996 Natl. Conf. Wood Transportation Structures, FPL-GTR-94*, USDA Forest Service, Forest Products Laboratory, Madison, Wis., 65–71.

Blankenhorn, P. R., Labosky, P. Jr., Janowiak, J. J., Manbeck, H. B., Webb, D. A, and Baileys, R. T. (1996). "Wood preservation—preservative treatment of hardwood glued–laminated bridges." *Proc., 1996 Natl. Conf. Wood Transportation Structures, FPL-GTR-94*, USDA Forest Service, Forest Products Laboratory, Madison, Wis., 261–269.

Boothby, T. E., Manbeck, H. B., Burroughs, C. B., Bernecker, C. A., Grgurevich, S., Cegelka, S., and Ritter, M. A. (1996). "Development of wood highway sound barriers." *Proc., 1996 Natl. Conf. Wood Transportation Structures, FPL-GTR-94*, USDA Forest Service, Forest Products Laboratory, Madison, Wis., 158–167.

Cesa, E., and Russell, K. (1996). "Wood in transportation program, technology transfer efforts." *Proc., 1996 Natl. Conf. Wood Transportation Structures, FPL-GTR-94*, USDA Forest Service, Forest Products Laboratory, Madison, Wis., 340–343.

Crawford, D. M., and DeGroot, R. C. (1996). "Evaluation of new creosote formulations." *Proc., 1996 Natl. Conf. Wood Transportation Structures, FPL-GTR-94*, USDA Forest Service, Forest Products Laboratory, Madison, Wis., 158–167.

Crews, K., and Bakoss, S. (1996). "Fundamental structural behavior of "built-up" stress laminated timber bridge decks." *Proc., 1996 Natl. Conf. Wood Transportation Structures, FPL-GTR-94*, USDA Forest Service, Forest Products Laboratory, Madison, Wis., 39–48.

Crews, K., Ritter, M., GangaRao, H., and Dickson, B. (1994). "State of the art research—stress-laminated timber bridge decks, Australia and North America." *Proc., 1994 Pacific Timber Engrg. Conf., Timber Research and Development Advisory Council*, Queensland, Australia, Vol. 2, 123–130.

Dagher, H. J., West, B., Caccese, V., Wolfe, R., and Ritter, M. (1996a). "Fatigue design criteria of MPC wood trusses for bridge applications." *Proc., 1996 Natl. Conf. Wood Transportation Structures, FPL-GTR-94*, USDA Forest Service, Forest Products Laboratory, Madison, Wis., 58–64.

Dagher, H. J., Kimball, T. E., Shaler, S. M., and Abdel–Mogid, B. (1996b). "Effect of FRP reinforcement on low grade eastern hemlock glulams." *Proc., 1996 Natl. Conf. Wood Transportation Structures, FPL-GTR-94*, USDA Forest Service, Forest Products Laboratory, Madison, Wis., 207–214.

Davalos, J. F., GangaRao, H. V. S., Sonti, S. S., Moody, R. C., and Hernandez, R. (1994). "Bulb-T and glulam-FRP beams from timber bridges." *Proc., 1994 Structures Congress*, Atlanta, Ga. ASCE 2, 1316–1321.

De Groot, R., Crawford, D., and Woodward, B. (1996). "Integrated efficacy evaluation of new preservatives in alternative wood species." *Proc., 1996 Natl. Conf. Wood Transportation Structures, FPL-GTR-94*, USDA Forest Service, Forest Products Laboratory, Madison, Wis., 379–388.

Dickson, B. (1996). "Engineered wood products for transportation structures—an overview of the obstacles and opportunities." *Proc., 1996 Natl. Conf. Wood Transportation Structures, FPL-GTR-94*, USDA Forest Service, Forest Products Laboratory, Madison, Wis., 490–494.

Dickson, B., and GangaRoa, H. (1990). "Development and testing of an experimental timber T-beam bridge." *Paper 89-0042*, U. S. Transportation Res. Board, Washington, D. C.

Duwadi, S. R., and Ritter, M. A. (1995). "Research on timber bridges and related topics." *Research Update*, Fed. Hwy. Admin., Washington, D. C.

Duwadi, S. R., and Wood, R. C. (1996). "The Federal Highway Administration timber bridge program." *Proc., 1996 Natl. Conf. Wood Transportation*

Structures, *FPL-GTR-94*, USDA Forest Service, Forest Products Laboratory, Madison, Wis., 333–339.

Faller, R. K., Rosson, B. T., Sicking, D. L., Ritter, M. A., and Bunnell, S. (1995). "Design and evaluation of two bridge railings for low-volume roads." *Proc., 6th Int. Conf. on Low-Volume Roads*, Minneapolis, MN. National Academy Press (2), 357–372.

Faller, R. K., Rosson, B. T., Ritter, M. A., Lee, P. D. H., and Duwadi, S. R. (1996). "Railing systems for longitudinal timber deck bridges." *Proc., 1996 Natl. Conf. Wood Transportation Structures*, *FPL-GTR-94*, USDA Forest Service, Forest Products Laboratory, Madison, Wis., 145–157.

Galloway, T. L., Fogstad, C., Dolan, C. W., and Puckett, J. A. (1996). "Initial tests of Kevlar prestressed timber beams." *Proc., 1996 Natl. Conf. Wood Transportation Structures*, *FPL-GTR-94*, USDA Forest Service, Forest Products Laboratory, Madison, Wis., 215–224.

Gopu, V. K. A. (1996). *Proceedings of 1996 InternationalWood Engineering Conference*, Dept. Civil Environ. Engrg., Louisiana State Univ. 4 vol.

Green, D. W., and McDonald, K. A. (1993). "Investigation of the mechanical properties of red oak 2 by 4's." *Wood Fiber Sci*, 25(1), 35–45.

Green, D. W., Ross, R. J., and McDonald, K. A. (1994). "Production of hardwood machine stress rated lumber." *Proc., 9th Int. Symp. Nondestructive Testing of Wood*, Forest Products Society, 141–150.

Green, D., Kretschmann, D., Wolcott, M.,and Ross, R. (1996). "Mechanical grading of timbers for transportation industry." *Proc., 1996 Natl. Conf. Wood Transportation Structures*, *FPL-GTR-94*, USDA Forest Service, Forest Products Laboratory, Madison, Wis., 186–191.

Gutkowski, R. M., and Williamson, T. G. (1984). "Heavy timber structures and bridges." *Proc., Structural Wood Research: State of the Art and Research Needs*, ASCE, 111–130.

Hernandez, R., Ritter, M. A., Moody, R. C., and Lee, P. D. H. (1996). "Yellow poplar glued–laminated timber: Product development and use in timber bridge construction." *Proc., 1996 Natl. Conf. Wood Transportation Structures*, *FPL-GTR-94*, USDA Forest Service, Forest Products Laboratory, Madison, Wis., 411–417.

Hislop, L. E. (1996). "Portable surfaces for crossing unstable roadbeds." *Proc., 1996 Natl. Conf. Wood Transportation Structures*, *FPL-GTR-94*, USDA Forest Service, Forest Products Laboratory, Madison, Wis., 138–144.

Hislop, L. E., and Ritter, M. A. (1996). "Field performance of timber bridges. 7. Connell Lake stress-laminated deck bridge." *Res. Pap. FPL-RP-550*, USDA Forest Service, Forest Products Laboratory, Madison, Wis.

Kainz, J. A., and Hill, C. A. (1996a). "McCurdy Road stress-laminated timber bridge: A viable option for short-span design." *Proc., 1996 Natl. Conf. Wood Transportation Structures*, *FPL-GTR-94*, USDA Forest Service, Forest Products Laboratory, Madison, Wis.,   418–426.

Kainz, J. A., Wacker, J. P., and Nelson, M. (1996b). "Field performance of timber bridges. 9. Big Erick's stress-laminated deck bridge." *Res. Pap. FPL-RP-552.* USDA Forest Service, Forest Products Laboratory, Madison, Wis.

Laks, P. E., Gutting, K. W., Pickens, J. B., and De Groot, R. C. (1996). "Field performance of new wood preservatives in secondary timber species." *Proc., 1996 Natl. Conf. Wood Transportation Structures, FPL-GTR-94,* USDA Forest Service, Forest Products Laboratory, Madison, Wis., 389–400.

Lee, P. D. H., and Wacker, J. P. (1996). "Standard plans for timber highway structures." *Proc., 1996 Natl. Conf. Wood Transportation Structures, FPL-GTR-94,* USDA Forest Service, Forest Products Laboratory, Madison, Wis., 344–350.

Lee, P. D. H., Ritter, M. A., and Triche, M. (1995). "Standard plans for Southern Pine bridges." *Gen. Tech. Rep. FPL-GTR-84.* USDA Forest Service, Forest Products Laboratory, Madison, Wis.

Lee, P. D. H., Ritter, M. A., and Tice, E. D. (1996a). "Eastern cottonwood stress-laminated timber bridges: Enhancing rural America with underutilized species." *Proc., 1996 Natl. Conf. Wood Transportation Structures, FPL-GTR-94,* USDA Forest Service, Forest Products Laboratory, Madison, Wis., 104–113.

Lee, P. D. H., Ritter, M. A., and Wacker, J. P. (1996b). "Field performance of timber bridges. 10. Sanborn Brook stress-laminated deck bridge." *Res. Pap. FPL-RP-555,* USDA Forest Service, Forest Products Laboratory, Madison, Wis.

Manbeck, H. B., Janowiak, J. J., Blankenhorn, P. R., Labosky, P., Moody, R. C., and Hernandez, R. (1993). "Red maple glulam timber beam performance." *Res. Pap. FPL-RP-519,* USDA Forest Service, Forest Products Laboratory, Madison, Wis.

Manbeck, H. B., Blankenhorn, P. R., Janowiak, J. J., Witmer, R. W. Jr., and Labosky, P. Jr. (1996a). "Performance of red oak and red maple glued–laminated bridges." *Proc., 1996 Natl. Conf. Wood Transportation Structures, FPL-GTR-94,* USDA Forest Service, Forest Products Laboratory, Madison, Wis., 82–91.

Manbeck, H. B., Janowiak, J. J, Blankenhorn, P. B., and Labosky, P. Jr. (1996b). "Standard designs for hardwood glued-laminated highway bridges." *Proc., 1996 Natl. Conf. Wood Transportation Structures, FPL-GTR-94,* USDA Forest Service, Forest Products Laboratory, Madison, Wis., 351–360.

Manbeck, H. B., Janowiak, J. J., Blankenhorn, P. B., Labosky, P. Jr., Moody, R. C., and Hernandez, R. (1996c). "Efficient hardwood glued–laminated beams." *Proc., 1996 Int. Wood Engrg.Conf.,* Dept. Civil Environ. Engrg., Louisiana State Univ., (1), 283–290.

McDonald, K. A., Green, D. W., Dwyer, J., and Whipple, J. W. (1993). "Red Maple stress-graded lumber from factory-grade logs." *Forest Prod. J.,* 43(11/12), 13–18.

McDonald, K. A., Hassler, C. C., Hawkins, J. E., and Pahl, T. L. (1996). "Hardwood structural lumber from log heart cants." *Forest Prod. J.,* 46(6), 55–62.

Moody, R. C., Hernandez, R., Davalos, J. F., and Sonti, S. S. (1993). "Yellow Poplar glulam timber beam performance." *Res. Pap. FPL-RP- 520*, USDA Forest Service, Forest Products Laboratory, Madison, Wis.

Pellerin, R. F., Lavinder, J. A., Ross, R. J., Falk, R. H., and Volny, N. (1996). "In-place detection of decay in timber bridges—An application of stress wave technology." *Proc., 1996 Natl. Conf. Wood Transportation Structures, FPL-GTR-94*, USDA Forest Service, Forest Products Laboratory, Madison, Wis., 282–291.

Rammer, D. R. (1996). "Shear strength of glued–laminated timber beams and panels." *Proc., 1996 Natl. Conf. Wood Transportation Structures, FPL-GTR-94*, USDA Forest Service, Forest Products Laboratory, Madison, Wis., 192–200.

Rammer, D. R., and McLean, D. I. (1996a). "Recent research on shear strength in wood beams." *Proc., 1996 Int. Wood Engrg. Conf.*, Dept. Civil Environ. Engrg., Louisiana State Univ. (2), 96–103.

Rammer, D. R., and McLean, D. I. (1996b). "Shear strength of wood beams." *Proc., 1996 Natl. Conf. Wood Transportation Structures, FPL-GTR-94*, USDA Forest Service, Forest Products Laboratory, Madison, Wis., 168–177.

Rammer, D. R., and Soltis, L.A. (1994). "Experimental shear strength of unchecked beams." *Res. Pap. FPL-RP-527*, USDA Forest Service, Forest Products Laboratory, Madison, Wis., 38 p.

Rammer, D. R., Soltis, L. A., and Lebow, P. K. (1996). "Experimental shear strength of solid-sawn Douglas-fir beams." *Res. Pap. FPL-RP-553*, USDA Forest Service, Forest Products Laboratory, Madison, Wis.

Ritter, M. A. (1990). "Timber bridges: Design, construction, inspection, and maintenance." *EM 7700-8*, U.S. Dept. Agric., Washington, D. C.

Ritter, M. A., and Lee, P. D. H. (1996). "Recommended construction practices for stress-laminated wood bridge decks". *Proc., 1996 Int. Wood Engrg. Conf.*, Dept. Civil Environ. Engrg., Louisiana State Univ. (1), 237–244.

Ritter, M. A., and Moody, R. C. (1991). "Timber bridge research by the USDA Forest Service, Forest Products Laboratory." *Proc., 1991 Int. Timber Engrg. Conf.*, Timber Res. Develop. Assoc., United Kingdom (3), 356–363.

Ritter, M., Moody, R., and Duwadi, S. (1994). "U.S. Timber bridge research." *Proc., PTEC 94*, Fortitude Valley MAC, Timber Res. Develop. Advisory Council, Queensland, Australia,(2), 148–155.

Ritter, M. A., Faller, R. K., Lee, P. D. H., Rosson, B. T., and Duwadi, S. R. (1995a). "Plans for crash-tested bridge railings for longitudinal wood decks." *Gen. Tech. Rep. FPL-GTR-87*, USDA Forest Service, Forest Products Laboratory, Madison, Wis.

Ritter, M. A., Wacker, J. P., and Tice, E.D. (1995b.) "Design, construction, and evaluation of timber bridge constructed of cottonwood lumber." *Proc., 4th Int. Bridge Engrg. Conf.*, National Academy Press, Washington, D.C., (2), 358–370.

Ritter, M. A., Wacker, J. P.,   and   Duwadi,   S. R.   (1995c.)   "Field performance of stress-laminated timber bridges on low-volume roads." *Proc., 6th Int. Conf. on Low-Volume Roads*, National Academy Press, Washington, D. C., (2), 347–357.

Ritter, M. A., Duwadi, S. R., and Lee, P. D. H. (1996a). *Proceedings of 1996 National Conference on Wood Transportation Structures, FPL-GTR-94*, USDA Forest Service, Forest Products Laboratory, Madison, Wis.

Ritter, M. A., Kainz, J. A., and Porter, G. J. (1996b). "Field performance of timber bridges. 5. Little Salmon Creek stress-laminated deck bridge." *Res. Pap. FPL-RP-547*, USDA Forest Service, Forest Products Laboratory, Madison, Wis.

Ritter, M., Lee, P. H., Kainz, J., and Meyer, C. (1996c.) "Evaluation of stress-laminated T-beam bridges constructed of laminated veneer lumber." *Proc., 1996 Natl. Conf. Wood Transportation Structures, FPL-GTR-94*, USDA Forest Service, Forest Products Laboratory, Madison, Wis., 92–103.

Ritter, M. A., Lee, P. D. H., and Porter, G. J. (1996d). "Field performance of timber bridges. 6. Hoffman Run stress-laminated deck bridge." *Res. Pap. FPL-RP-549*. USDA Forest Service, Forest Products Laboratory, Madison, Wis.

Ritter, M. A., Moody, R. C., and Duwadi, S. R. (1996e.) "Summary of U.S. research on wood transportation structures." *Proc., 1996 Int. Wood Engrg. Conf.*, Dept. Civil Environ. Engrg., Louisiana State University, (1), 81–88.

Ross, R. J., Ritter, M. A., and Schad, K. C. (1996.) "Determining in-place modulus of elasticity of stress-laminated timber decks using NDE." *Res. Pap. FPL-RP-547*, USDA Forest Service, Forest Products Laboratory, Madison, Wis., 277–281.

Soltis, L. A., and Rammer, D.R. (1994.) "Shear strength of unchecked glue–laminated beams." *Forest Prod. J.*, 44(1), 1–8.

Sonti, S. S., Davalos, J. F., Hernandez, R., Moody, R. C., and Kim, Y. (1995). "Laminated wood beams reinforced with pultruded fiber-reinforced plastic." *Proc., Composites Inst. 50th Annual Conf. and Expo '95*, SPI Composites Institute, New York.

Taylor, S. E., and Ritter, M. A. (1996). "Portable T-section bridge for low-volume roads." *Res. Pap. FPL-RP-547*, USDA Forest Service, Forest Products Laboratory, Madison, Wis., 426–436.

Taylor, S. E., Ritter, M. A., Keliher, K. P., and Thompson, J. D. (1996). "Portable glulam timber bridge systems." *Proc., 1996 Int. Wood Engrg. Conf.*, Dept. Civil Environ. Engrg., Louisiana State Univ., (2), 368–375.

Thomas, W. R., and Puckett, J. A. (1996.) "Analysis, design, rating, and drafting of wood bridge superstructures." *Proc., 1996 Natl. Conf. Wood Transportation Structures, FPL-GTR-94*, USDA Forest Service, Forest Products Laboratory, Madison, Wis., 361–370.

Tingley, D. A. (1990). "Predicting strength criteria for Kevlar and fiberglass reinforced plastic (KRP and FRP) glued laminated beams." *Proc., Int. Timber Engrg. Conf.*, Tokyo, Japan, (1), 42–45.

Tingley, D. A, and Cegelka, S. (1996). "High-strength-fiber-reinforced plastic-reinforced wood." *Proc., 1996 Int. Wood Engrg. Conf.,* Dept. Civil Environ. Engrg., Louisiana State Univ., Baton Rouge, (3), 57–66.

Triche, M. H., and Ritter, M. A. (1996). "Pole Creek metal-plate-connected truss bridge." *Proc., 1996 Natl. Conf. Wood Transportation Structures, FPL-GTR-94,* USDA Forest Service, Forest Products Laboratory, Madison, Wis., 49–57.

Wacker, J. P., and Ritter, M. A. (1992). "Field performance of timber bridges. 1. Teal River stress-laminated deck bridge." *Res. Pap. FPL-RP-515,* USDA Forest Service, Forest Products Laboratory, Madison, Wis.

Wacker, J. P., and Ritter, M. A. (1995a). "Field performance of timber bridges. 3. Birchlog Run and Tumbling Rock Run stress-laminated deck bridges." *Res. Pap. FPL-RP-538,* USDA Forest Service, Forest Products Laboratory, Madison, Wis.

Wacker, J. P., and Ritter, M. A. (1995b). "Field performance of timber bridges. 4. Graves Crossing stress-laminated deck bridge." *FPL- RP-539,* USDA Forest Service, Forest Products Laboratory, Madison, Wis.

Wacker, J. P., Ritter, M. A., and Conger, D. (1996). "Field performance of timber bridges. 8. Lynches Woods Park stress-laminated deck bridge." *Res. Pap. FPL-RP-551,* USDA Forest Service, Forest Products Laboratory, Madison, Wis..

Wang, J. Z., and De Groot, R. (1996). "Treatability and durability of heartwood." *Proc., 1996 Natl. Conf. Wood Transportation Structures, FPL-GTR-94,* USDA Forest Service, Forest Products Laboratory, Madison, Wis., 252–260.

Wipf, T. J., Ritter, M. A., Duwadi, S. R., and Moody, R. C. (1993). "Development of six-year research needs assessment for timber transportation structures." *Gen. Tech. Rep. FPL-GTR-74,* USDA Forest Service, Forest Products Laboratory, Madison, Wis.

Wipf, T. J., Ritter, M. A., and Wood, D. L. (1996). "Dynamic evaluation of timber bridges." *Proc., 1996 Natl. Conf. Wood Transportation Structures, FPL-GTR-94,* USDA Forest Service, Forest Products Laboratory, Madison, Wis., 114–121.

Wolfe, R. W., and Gjinolli, A. E. (1996). "Assessment of cement-bonded wood composites as a means of using low-valued wood for engineering applications." *Proc., 1996 Int. Wood Engrg. Conf.,* Dept. Civil Environ. Engrg., Louisiana State Univ., Baton Rouge, (3), 74–81.

Design Specifications and Standards

John "Buddy" Showalter, P.E., MASCE[1]

Abstract

A transition to performance-based codes and load and resistance factor design (LRFD) in the U.S. will shape research needs for wood products into the 21st century.

Introduction

With the advent of the International Codes Council™ (ICC) and its development of the *International Building Code™* (IBC), code groups are looking to incorporate performance-based code provisions into the proposed new single national U.S. building code. Models such as the United Kingdom Code and the New Zealand Code are being studied to determine how best to make the transition in the U.S.

Now that the wood industry has developed a *Standard for Load and Resistance Factor Design (LRFD) for Engineered Wood Construction*, AF&PA/ASCE 16-95, the transition to LRFD will begin, as well. Already, several timber engineering courses in the U.S. are utilizing the new methodology, which is critical for engineering students who are only being taught LRFD for steel and concrete. The LRFD format, which is a form of reliability based design, will provide a more realistic and rational approach for incorporating new research on materials and loads.

Building Codes

Design specifications and standards for wood products have been developed on a national level in the United States since the early 1900s. Standards become enforceable by law when they are adopted into the building codes. There are several organizations in the U.S. that develop model building codes. These organizations and their respective model codes are:

◆   Building Officials and Code Administrators, International (BOCA), which develops the *National Building Code* (1996);

◆   Southern Building Code Congress, International (SBCCI), which develops the

---

[1]   Manager, Technology Transfer, American Forest & Paper Association, 1111 19th Street, NW, Suite 800, Washington, DC 20036

Standard Building Code (1997); and
♦   International Conference of Building Officials (ICBO), which develops the
        Uniform Building Code™ (1997).

In recent years these model code organizations formed an organization called the
International Codes Council, with a goal of developing the *International Building Code*
for publication in the year 2000. If successful, this effort could result in a single national
building code in the U.S.

Performance Based Codes

One of the subcommittees of the ICC is the Performance Based Code (PBC)
Technical Subcommittee, whose function is to foster opportunities for performance-
based criteria in the IBC. At a recent workshop sponsored by the PBC, several groups
provided insight into the emergence of PBCs in the U.S. A representative of the National
Institute of Science and Technology (NIST), stated that it was NIST's intent to interact
with the enforcement community as the U.S. moves forward with the development of
PBCs. To do this NIST will try to develop technology to implement PBCs.

A representative of the Society of Fire Protection Engineers (SFPE) stated that
performance codes are inevitable and that 90%-95% of buildings will be built to
performance standards in the future. The United Kingdom Code has shown this to be
true with their PBC and deemed-to-satisfy criteria. According to SFPE, a *Design Guide
Frame Work Document for Engineering Standards and Practice* is being developed.
SFPE also has a publication on *Evaluation of Performance Based Codes and Fire Safety
Design Methods.*

The International Fire Chiefs Institute (IFCI), has a Performance Based
Technical Subcommittee with two common goals. The first being to link prescriptive
with performance based design. The second, to establish a top-down versus bottom-up
approach.

Building officials in Clark County, Nevada, probably have the most practical
experience with performance based codes in the U.S., and already use performance
based criteria to build most of the large hotels and entertainment centers in Las Vegas.

Already, several countries around the world have introduced performance based
codes. The New Zealand Building Code, for example, specifies performance with a five
level structure, as follows:

1.   Objective,
2.   Functional requirement,
3.   Performance,
4.   Verification method,
5.   Acceptable solution (Buchanan, 1994).

An example of performance criteria from the New Zealand Building Code

(1992) is as follows (words in italics are terms defined in the NZ Building Code):

Clause C4 - Structural Stability During Fire

Objective
C4.1   The objective of this provision is to:
  (a)   safeguard people from injury due to loss of structural stability during *fire*, and
  (b)   protect *household units* and *other property* from damage due to structural instability caused by *fire*.

Functional Requirement
C4.2   *Buildings* shall be constructed to maintain structural stability during a fire to:
  (a)   allow people *adequate* time to evacuate safely,
  (b)   allow fire service personnel *adequate* time to undertake rescue and firefighting operations, and
  (c)   avoid collapse and consequential damage to adjacent *household units* or *other property*.

Performance
C4.3.1   Structural elements of *buildings* shall have *fire* resistance appropriate to the function of the elements, the *fire load*, the *fire intensity*, the *fire hazard*, the height of the *buildings* and the *fire* control facilities external to and within them.
C4.3.2   Structural elements shall have a *fire* resistance of no less than that of any element to which they provide support within the same *firecell*.
C4.3.3   Collapse of elements having lesser *fire* resistance shall not cause the consequential collapse of elements required to have a higher *fire* resistance (Buchanan, 1994).

Research to support performance based codes should lead to development of design tools a fire protection engineer can use to meet performance objectives or goals. Characterizing flame spread performance of materials and modeling structural performance under fire are two examples of the type of research that can lead to development of appropriate tools.

It is clear that worldwide performance based codes will be a reality in the 21st century. Wood products stand to benefit tremendously from an approach that sets performance criteria rather than prescriptive, as the standard. This will level the playing field with other competing materials in the construction marketplace. Research in the area of fire performance of wood products, especially, could provide enormous progress for wood products in a performance based code arena.

LRFD versus ASD

Publication of the *Standard for Load and Resistance Factor Design (LRFD) for Engineered Wood Construction*, AF&PA/ASCE 16-95, culminated nearly two decades of development by the wood industry. Already, the transition to LRFD has begun, as several timber engineering courses in the U.S. are utilizing the new methodology. This is critical for the viability of wood design in the U.S. as engineering students are almost exclusively being taught LRFD for steel and concrete (Marx 1996).

However, the transition from allowable stress design (ASD) to LRFD took approximately two decades for the concrete industry and is over 10 years for steel. Informal surveys of designers during educational design seminars indicates an overwhelming desire on the part of practicing engineers to maintain ASD procedures. Therefore, the wood industry intends to maintain both ASD, in the form of the *National Design Specification® (NDS®) for Wood Construction* (1991), and LRFD for the foreseeable future.

The wood industry chose soft conversion from ASD to make transition to LRFD as straightforward as possible. So, results using LRFD should be within ±10% of results using ASD (Pollock and Williamson 1994).

The primary motivation for switching to LRFD is the ability to more accurately quantify material strengths based on statistical methods. This will give designers more confidence in the "reliability" of their designs. This will also better enable research results to be utilized for both material properties and loads.

Research in the 21st century will have to account for the fact that both ASD and LRFD will coexist, at least short-term. Long term, the focus of research should be to characterize ultimate capacities of materials. Serviceability considerations will continue to require attention as well.

Standards Development Groups

As workshop participants meet to discuss strategy for research in the next century, it might be of value to understand the scope of the standards development for wood products. There are a number of groups in the U.S. that develop standards for wood products, or standards that affect the use of wood products. Table 1 lists standards developers with their respective standards that appear in one or more of the current model building codes. For the purpose of this paper, standards are categorized as either design (Table 1A), quality (Table 1B), or material property development (Table 1C).

Specific Research Needs

The author is currently aware of two organizations in the wood industry that have prioritized research needs. Table 2A and 2B outline structural and fire research needs, respectively, as developed by the Technical Committee of the American Forest & Paper Association. Tables 3A and 3B outline research needs for glulam and for other products affecting the use of glulam as developed by the Research Task Committee of the American Institute of Timber Construction. Some of these items obviously overlap with other working groups of the research workshop, but it is hoped that by incorporating them here, they will be available for review and discussion by pertinent groups.

Conclusion

From a research standpoint, transition to performance based codes and LRFD are the most significant changes facing the wood industry as the 21st century approaches. Research in the area of fire performance of wood products, especially, could provide enormous progress for wood products in a performance based code arena. Research will also have to account for the fact that both ASD and LRFD for wood will coexist in the near future. Long term, the focus of research should be to characterize ultimate capacities of materials, while not neglecting serviceability considerations.

References

1.   Buchanan, A.H. *Fire Engineering for a Performance Based Code*. Fire Safety Journal 23 (1994) 1-16. Elsevier Science Limited. 1994.

2.   *Design Guide Frame Work Document for Engineering Standards and Practice*. Society of Fire Protection Engineers. Boston, MA. Draft.

3.   *Evaluation of Performance Based Codes and Fire Safety Design Methods*. Society of Fire Protection Engineers. Boston, MA.

4.   Marx, C.M. *Wood Engineering Education in the U.S.* Proceedings of the International Wood Engineering Conference. Omnipress. 1996.

5.   *National Building Code*. Building Officials and Code Administrators, International. Country Club Hills, IL. 1996.

6.   Pollock, D. G. and T.G. Williamson. *LRFD vs. ASD for Wood Structures*. Proceedings of the IASS-ASCE International Symposium on Spatial, Lattice and Tension Structures. American Society of Civil Engineers. 1994.

7.   *National Design Specification (NDS) for Wood Construction*. American Forest & Paper Association. Washington, DC. 1991.

8.   New Zealand Building Code Handbook and Approved Documents. Building Industry Authority. Wellington, New Zealand. 1992.

9.   *Standard Building Code*. Southern Building Code Congress, International. Birmingham, AL. 1997.

10.   *Standard for Load and Resistance Factor Design (LRFD) for Engineered Wood Construction*, AF&PA/ASCE 16-95. American Society of Civil Engineers. New York, NY. 1996.

11.   *Uniform Building Code*. International Conference of Building Officials. Whittier, CA. 1997.

Table 1A. **Standards Developers and Design Standards for Wood Products or Affecting Wood Products in the U.S.**

DESIGN STANDARDS	
Standards Organization	**Standard(s)**
American Forest & Paper Association (AF&PA)	ANSI/AF&PA NDS-91 *National Design Specification® (NDS®) for Wood Construction*
	AF&PA/ASCE 16-95 *Standard for Load and Resistance Factor Design (LRFD) for Engineered Wood Construction*
	Wood Frame Construction Manual for One- and Two-Family Dwellings, SBC High Wind Edition (WFCM-SBC)
	Design Fabrication and Installation of Permanent Wood Foundations
American Institute of Timber Construction (AITC)	AITC 104: Typical Construction Details
	AITC 112: Standard for Tongue-and Groove Heavy Timber Roof Decking
	AITC 190.1: Structural Glued Laminated Timber
American National Standards Institute (ANSI)	A05.1-1972 Wood Poles
	A208.1-93 Particleboard
American Society of Agricultural Engineers (ASAE)	EP486 Post and Pole Foundation Design
American Society of Civil Engineers (ASCE)	ASCE 7-95 *Minimum Design Loads for Buildings and Other Structures*
APA-The Engineered Wood Association	*Plywood Design Specification* Supp. 1 - Design & Fabrication of Plywood Curved Panels Supp. 2 - Design & Fabrication of Plywood-Lumber beams Supp. 3 - Design & Fabrication of Plywood Stressed-Skin Panels Supp. 4 - Design & Fabrication of Plywood Sandwich Panels Supp. 5 - Design & Fabrication of All-Plywood Beams
National Fire Protection Association (NFPA) *[Note: this is not a comprehensive list of NFPA Standards, but is intended to provide a broad overview]*	NFPA 220 Standard Building Types and Definitions NFPA 221 Fire Walls and Fire Barrier Walls NFPA 80A Protection of Buildings from Exterior Fire Exposures NFPA 299 Protection of Life and Property from Wildfire NFPA 251 Fire Test of Building Construction and Materials NFPA 255 Test of Surf. Burning Characteristics of Bldg Materials NFPA 264 Heat Release of Oxygen Consumption Calorimeter NFPA 101 Life Safety Code
National Institute of Building Sciences (NIBS)	Building Seismic Safety Council (BSSC) *National Earthquake Hazard Reduction Provisions (NEHRP)*
Truss Plate Institute (TPI)	TPI 1-1995 *National Design Standard for Metal Plate Connected Wood Trusses*

Table 1B.   **Standards Developers and Quality Standards for Wood Products or Affecting Wood Products in the U.S.**

QUALITY	
Standards Organization	**Standard(s)**
American Institute of Timber Construction (AITC)	AITC 200: Inspection Manual
American Society of Heating, Refrigeration, and Air Conditioning Engineers (ASHRAE)	ANSI/ASHRAE 62-1989 Ventilation for Acceptable Indoor Air Quality
American Wood Preservers Association (AWPA)	C1, C2, C3, C4, C9, C14, C15, C16, C22, C23, C24, C28 and M4, for species, product, preservative and end use. Preservatives shall conform to AWPA P1/P13, P2, P5, P8 and P9.
Hardwood Plywood and Veneer Association (HPVA)	HP-1-94 Hardwood and Decorative Plywood

Table 1C.   **Standards Developers and Material Property Standards for Wood Products or Affecting Wood Products in the U.S.**

MATERIAL PROPERTY DEVELOPMENT	
Standards Organization	**Standard(s)**
American Hardboard Association (AHA)	A135.4-95 Basic Hardboard
	A135.6-90 Hardboard Siding
	A194.1-85 Cellulosic Fiber Board
American Institute of Timber Construction (AITC)	AITC 110: Standard Appearance Grades for Structural Glued Laminated Timber
	AITC 113: Standard for Dimensions of Structural Glued Laminated Timber
	AITC 117: Structural Glued-laminated Timber
	AITC 119: Standard Specifications for Hardwood Glued-Laminated Timber
	AITC 500: Tests for Structural Glued-laminated Timber
American Society of Agricultural Engineers (ASAE)	EP388.2 Design Properties of Round, Sawn and Laminated Preservatively Treated Construction Poles and Posts
ASTM D-07 on Wood *[Note: this is not a comprehensive list of D07 Standards, but is intended to provide a broad overview]*	D1990 Practice for Establishing Allowable Properties for Visually Graded Dimension Lumber from In-Grade Tests of Full-Size Specimens D2899 Method for Establishing Design Stresses for Round Timber Piles D3043 Methods for Testing Structural Panels in Flexure D3737 Test Method for Establishing Stresses for Structural Glued-Laminated Timber (Glulam) D5055 Specification for Establishing and Monitoring Structural Capacities of Prefabricated Wood I-joists D5456 Specification for Evaluation of Structural Composite Lumber D5457 Specification for Computing the Reference Resistance of Wood-Based Materials and Structural Connections for Load and Resistance Factor Design D5652 Test Methods for Bolted Connections in Wood and Wood-Base Products

Table 1C (cont'd).   **Standards Developers and Material Property Standards for Wood Products or Affecting Wood Products in the U.S.**

MATERIAL PROPERTY DEVELOPMENT	
Standards Organization	**Standard(s)**
ASTM E-05 on Fire	E119 Standard Test Methods for Fire Tests of Building Construction and Materials
ASTM E-6 on Building Construction	E72-95 Methods of Conducting Strength Tests of Panels for Building Construction E84-95b Test Method for Surface Burning Characteristics of Building Materials E6.66 subcommittee on a *Performance Based Residential Building Code.*
ASTM E-50 on Environmental Performance	Subcommittee E50.06 on Green Buildings.
ASTM F-16 on Fasteners	F1575-95 Standard Test Method for Determining Bending Yield Moment of Nails
	F1667 Specification for Driven Fasteners: Nails, Spikes and Staples
Hardwood Plywood and Veneer Association (HPVA)	HP-SG-86 Structural Design Guide for Hardwood Plywood Wall Panels
U.S. Department of Commerce	PS 1-95 Construction and Industrial Plywood
	PS 2-95 Performance Standard for Wood-Based Structural-Use Panels
	PS 20-94 American Softwood Lumber Standard

Table 2A.   American Forest & Paper Association Structural Research Needs

Rank	HIGH PRIORITY
1	Type IV Walls Design Methodology - Perform additional shearwall tests and develop design procedure to account for the combined uplift and shear resistance of walls sheathed with structural sheathing.
2	Performance of Wood Structures and Components Under Extreme Wind Loading - Partial funding to the University of Western Ontario to conduct MWFRS and C&C load correlations to be used in the design of light-framing design.
	MEDIUM PRIORITY
3	Energy-Based Seismic Design - Develop "Energy-Based" seismic design procedures for wood products and assemblies which will account for ductility these systems.
4	Notching Design - Develop design procedure to account for the effects of notching on bending and shear strength for possible inclusion in *NDS* & *AF&PA/ASCE-16.*
	LOW PRIORITY
5	Cyclic Lag Screw and Wood Screw Testing - Conduct cyclic testing of lag screws and wood screws.
6	Dowel Bearing Strength Properties - Develop dowel-bearing strength properties for materials used in wood design and construction including gypsum, fiberboard, hardboard, and OSB.

Table 2B.   American Forest & Paper Association Fire Research Needs

Rank	HIGH PRIORITY
1	Two-Dimensional Pyrolysis Model - Complete the one-dimensional pyrolysis model and develop a two-dimensional model.
	MEDIUM PRIORITY
2	Structural & Thermal Effects - Analyze and characterize structural and thermal effects occurring in floor assembly fire tests.
3	Floor Assembly Fire Tests - Conduct floor assembly fire test to validate fire endurance of wood frame floor assemblies.
4	Heavy Timber Compression & Tension Tests - Conduct fire tests of heavy timber columns and tension members.
	LOW PRIORITY
5	ASTM E84 Flame Spread Testing - Determine the flame spread index for the 7 materials that are tested in the Cone calorimeter and ICAL, to establish a basis for comparison with degrees of combustibility.
6	NFPRF ICAL Project - Fund second year of National Fire Protection Research Foundation ICAL project.

Table 3A. American Institute of Timber Construction Glulam Research Needs

Rank	Project	Weighting (1-20 scale)	Priority
1.	End joints. ► NDT for end joint quality ► Proof test methods ► Economical high strength end joints ► Qualification levels ► FRP ► Evaluation of existing data ► Other products affected: I-Joist, trusses	16.3	High
2.	Laminating effect ► Planning laminations prior to wide-face gluing - affect on load sharing ► Presurfacing ► European method (1.25)	12	Medium
3.	Material properties ► Complete material property database needed for glulam models ► Test standards to facilitate technology transfer ► Tracking the resource ► Enlarging database for foreign species and new hardwoods ► Missing properties for certain species (i.e., end joints) ► In-grade - review available data ► On going knot survey (SG, E, h, xbar) ► "302" tension lumber	12.9	Medium
4.	Design procedures for glulam members and systems ► Simplify arch design - computer model ► Buckling - appropriate stability factors	7.2	Low
5.	Volume effect ► Definition ► Species differences ► Effect on MOR ► Effect on shear strength ► Effect on FRP ► Lumber versus glulam discrepancy	13.7	Medium

Table 3A (cont'd).   American Institute of Timber Construction Glulam Research Needs

Rank	Project	Weighting (1-20 scale)	Priority
6.	Stochastic glulam timber model(s) ▸ Expand to include tension, compression and shear properties ▸ Update fire performance models - 2 hour ▸ Standard (ASTM) on glulam modeling (technology transfer) ▸ Performance levels and implementation	11.1	Medium
7.	Wane lumber for glulam manufacture ▸ Bridge deck applications	10.3	Medium
8.	Compression wood ▸ degree of damage ▸ identification	7.6	Low

Table 3B.   American Institute of Timber Construction Research Needs Affecting Glulam

Rank	Project	Weighting (1-20 scale)	Priority
1.	Connections ▸ Evaluate behavior of multiple fastener connections - fabrication tolerances ▸ Study failure mechanisms of common connection systems ▸ Nails ▸ Glulam rivets ▸ Reduced bearing plate thickness (beam hangers & arch base shoes) ▸ Coupling fastener loads and beam bearing or increasing compression perp tolerance ▸ FRP	16.4	High
2.	Design procedures for members and systems ▸ Evaluate notch design procedures ▸ Tension perpendicular to grain	8.7	Low
3.	Fire rating calculation for heavy timber decking	6.4	Low
4.	Environmentally acceptable preservative treatments ▸ Field treating	12.1	Medium
5.	In-situ nondestructive evaluation techniques (NDT) ▸ Standardization ▸ Decay detection and subsequent strength assessment ▸ Connections	11.9	Medium
6.	Design ratings for heavy timber decking	5.9	Low
7.	Reducing condensation in "cold" wood framed roof installations	7.6	Low
8.	Building systems approach ▸ Arches and decking	7.4	Low

RESEARCH ON WOOD ENGINEERING:
AN INTERNATIONAL PERSPECTIVE

R.H. Leicester[1]

Abstract

This paper reviews current research trends related to timber engineering in countries outside of North America, and specifically considers the trends in Europe, Australasia, Japan, South Africa and tropical countries. Topics in fundamental research are noted. In addition it found that for reasons of technology transfer and of trade, there is a strong motivation to develop performance criteria for comparing existing products and assessing new products; the latter include not only criteria for in-service performance, but also criteria for the assessment of strength under long duration loads and under biodeterioration conditions. Finally the trend towards the globalisation of timber engineering leads to special technology for harmonising the existing performance standards of various countries and for the drafting of globally applicable international standards.

Introduction

The purpose of this paper is to review current research and development trends related to timber engineering and to extrapolate these trends towards the future. Developments related to the production of structural materials will not be reviewed, although these obviously will have a strong influence on the future of timber engineering. Also developments within the North American continent will not be reviewed, as these will be discussed in other papers at this Workshop.

Useful sources of information on international trends can be found in the popular international Conferences that have been convened during the past decade. These took place at Auckland (1984, 1989), Seattle (1988), Tokyo (1990), London (1991), Gold Coast (1994) and New Orleans (1996).

Most of the international research focuses on to the design of simple structural elements and the drafting of standards for assessing the design properties

---

[1] Chief Research Scientist, CSIRO Building, Construction and Engineering, Melbourne, Australia

of these elements. However, increasingly there is research related to quality control matters, to the design of structural assemblies (such as floor systems) and to design concepts for total buildings and other constructed facilities.

North America

The timber engineering research undertaken in North America provides a very useful starting point for research undertaken elsewhere. The reasons for this are the comprehensive and logical structure of the research (arising probably from legal and regulatory pressures), the targeting of this research for immediate industry application and the extensive publication of the research results.

Much of this research is undertaken at research centres with major concentrations of expertise, such as the Forest Products Laboratory at Wisconsin and the UBC/Forintek centre at Vancouver. In addition, the numerous ASTM Standards have proved extremely useful. For much of this research immediate industrial applications are made by industry associations such as the Council of Forest Industries, the Western Wood Products Association and the APA - Engineered Wood Association.

Europe

European research is comprehensively covered in the documentation of CIB-W18, a CIB working group that tends to concentrate on assessing research information for use in design codes and standards related to timber engineering. Since 1973 the working group has held about one meeting a year, the last three being held in Sydney, Australia (July 1994), Copenhagen, Denmark (April 1995) and Bordeaux, France (August 1996). The extent of research covered by CIB-W18 is indicated by the fact that the proceedings of the workshops to date contain more than 650 papers in 25 topic areas. Other sources of information on European research are the IUFRO/S5.02 Timber Engineering Workshops, and the workshops of some of the RILEM working groups.

During the past decade, research in Europe has been driven by the desire to publish a unified timber engineering design code, Eurocode 5, and a comprehensive set of related CEN Standards for classifying material properties. The extensive nature of this work has resulted in the European documents being used as the first draft of many ISO standards.. Associated with this was the development of a teaching package named 'STEP', an acronym for Structural Timber Education Programme (Blass 1996). Implementation of the STEP program cost 1.6 million ECU, involved 14 countries and 50 authors.

In addition to the above, a major collaborative research project titled 'COST 508' was undertaken to study the fundamentals of Wood Mechanics. COST is a framework for scientific cooperation between European countries. It is funded through the Commission of European Communities. During 1990 to 1996, COST

508 organised 6 workshops, involving 71 laboratories from 18 countries of Western and Eastern Europe.

Fundamental problems on wood mechanics that are of current interest in Europe include fracture mechanics, mechano-sorptive creep, load duration on strength, fatigue strength and the comparative properties of juvenile and mature wood. Properties of structural lumber, structural glues, glulam and board materials are important. Work on connectors includes evaluation procedures for conventional joints, together with methods for developing new strong joints such as through the use of epoxy-glued steel dowels.

Current research on machine stress grading is motivated largely by a desire to improve the output of higher grade material for glulam. In addition to the conventional mechanical grading systems, studies are being made on the use of microwave, laser and x-ray scanning equipment. There is also a continuing effort at developing effective design criteria for the dynamic characteristics of floors. Of particular interest is the proposal to construct and load test a 5-storey timber frame building at Cardington, United Kingdom (Enjily and Mettam 1995, Mettam et al 1996). Among other matters, the full size building will be tested to evaluate strength, accidental damage, serviceability, fire resistance and construction aspects.

Finally, mention should be made of the amazing and innovative structural timber designs of European engineers/architects such as J. Natterer, N. Torp, H. Bruninghoff and K. Linkwitz. While outside the scope of conventional code-controlled design, the work of these brilliant practitioners may eventually lead to a new and exciting branch of engineering science.

Australia/New Zealand

The timber engineering technology of Australia and New Zealand has always developed collaboratively, and even more so in the past few years since the signing of a memorandum of understanding to develop joint codes and standards. Useful reference sources for examining progress in research for these countries are the proceedings of the Forest Products Research Conference, held every two or three years. The last one was the 25th Conference, held in Melbourne in 1996. Additional information may be obtained from the proceedings of the Pacific Timber Engineering Conferences held in Auckland (1984, 1989) and the Gold Coast (1994).

The major timber resources in Australia and New Zealand are monoculture softwood plantation and mixed species hardwood forests.

Radiata pine is the predominant softwood grown in plantations. Typically the trees are felled at 30-40 years age. The production and utilisation technology is very similar to that of North America. However a greater proportion, about 90 percent, is mechanically stress graded; currently there is extensive research being undertaken to develop methods to control the quality of machine-graded timber (Leicester 1994, 1996).

The hardwoods utilised are predominantly medium-density eucalyptus species, felled at 40-70 years age; air dry density is 600-800 kg/m^3 . Relative to the softwoods, these hardwoods are difficult to process and to use; the sawn timber tends to distort and twist due to the effects of growth stresses; it is slow to air dry, difficult to nail and glue, and structural members tend to be heavy to handle. However these hardwoods have high strength, typically 2-3 times that of the softwoods.

For both the hardwood and softwood species, new methods of structural grading and new structural grades are continually being developed. The motivation for this is often to obtain maximum efficiency in exploiting a resource that is unique and is available only to a particular producer or group of producers. The grading methods developed are either new visual grades or a hybrid combination of visual and machine grading; the procedures used are outside the scope of conventional visual and machine grading as specified in the Australian standards AS:2082, AS:2858 and AS:1748 (Standards Australia 1979, 1986a and 1978); all grades of timber produced are assessed according to the in-grade testing procedures specified in AS/NZS:4063 (Standards Australia/Standards New Zealand 1992).

The natural forests of Australia contain many species of timber, the eucalypts alone comprising some 700 species; the Australian Standard AS:2878 (Standards Australia 1986a) lists the strength properties of about 350 species. The various difficulties associated with utilising multiple species is compounded by the fact that the properties of timber from regrowth forests, such as those that arise after major bushfires, are quite different from those of the timber from mature forests. Currently structural grading of timber within Australia and New Zealand requires species or species mixture identification. Earlier attempts to develop technology for the structural grading of mixtures of unidentified species, such as that given in the Australian Standard on "proof-grading", AS:3519 (Standards Australia 1993) have not been progressed in recent years.

In terms of basic structural elements, topics of current research in Australia and New Zealand include the strength of finger jointed timber (particularly the reliability of finger joint strength in seasoned hardwood and in unseasoned softwood timbers), the long duration strength of melamine fortified urea formaldehyde glued joints (particularly when used in the tropical areas of Australia) and mechano-sorptive effects. There is concern with joint systems for large structural elements (including epoxy-glued steel-dowel joints); in New Zealand the particular concern is with the earthquake resistance of these joints. There is also an active collaboration with North America in the development of Stress-Lam bridge technology (Crews and Walter 1996).

A strong unifying theme in current research is the endeavour to move away from prescriptive standards and to move towards in-service performance and function criteria. The difficulty is to develop suitable verification criteria for this purpose.

One attempt to assess the function of structural design occurred some years ago when a safety analysis of Australian structural design codes was undertaken

(Leicester et al 1986), somewhat similar to that which had been done for the design codes of USA (Ellingwood et al 1980). However the most successful application of performance based criteria to date has been to argue successfully for the removal of some traditional combustibility requirements that used to exist within the Building Code of Australia (Appleton 1993, Leicester 1995). Application of the risk analysis associated with this topic is now the subject of a multi million dollar Fire Code Reform project.

Another major research project related to performance criteria is to develop a general standard for assessing all types of structural joints. In this standard, each joint system will be considered to be an unknown "black box"; the focus will be on the specification of loading criteria that realistically simulate in-service loading conditions; these loading conditions are planned to include floor live loads, thunderstorm and cyclonic wind loads, and earthquake loads. It is expected that one spin-off from this standard will be another standard that is suitable for application in whole-house testing such as that undertaken at the James Cook University Cyclone Testing Station (Reardon and Henderson 1996).

Current research related to performance criteria are also being pursued with respect to the assessment of the strength of composite steel-timber assemblies, the dynamic behaviour of floor systems and the strength of timber products under long duration load. With respect to the last topic, it is of interest to note that an international workshop to discuss methods for assessing the long term strength of board material was convened in Toronto in 1993 by the Structural Board Association of North America; however no agreement on a test protocol was obtained at that meeting.

Finally mention should be made of an ambitious industry-sponsored project to develop an engineering approach to the design of structures to resist attack by decay, termite activity, corrosion and climate effects. This three-year project is spread across several organisations (McKenzie 1996). A pivotal feature of the project is to develop a probabilistic model to predict loss of strength, serviceability and aesthetic values (Leicester 1996).

Japan

Information on current trends in Japan can be obtained from the international conferences cited earlier, and in particular the International Timber Engineering Conference held in Tokyo in 1990.

A major part of the research in Japan is related to earthquake resistant design and in particular to the behaviour of shear walls and joint systems. Much of this research has an experimental base due to the fact that the unique structural system to be found in the traditional Japanese houses means that the results of North American research are not easily applied here. There are several large scale test facilities in Japan, and accordingly much of the research is in the form of full size and whole house testing.

An important influence on current research is recent government policy aimed at deregulation of the building industry. One aspect of this has been an attempt to reduce technical barriers to trade through the harmonisation of Japanese standards with those of ISO and other countries. As a result there has been an increased focus on performance based criteria which are seen to be a vehicle for pursuing deregulation and harmonisation.

South Africa

Information on research trends in South Africa can be obtained from the international conferences cited earlier and also on the proceeding of an international conference held in Pretoria in 1985 titled "Forest Products Research International-Achievements and the Future".

In general the research trends tend to follow those of North America. However there has been a special interest in the development of low cost mechanical stress-grading machines (Vinopal 1985), roof truss design, epoxy-glued steel dowel joints, and reinforced glulam made from eucalyptus species.

Tropical Countries

Tropical countries that grow and utilise timber for structural purposes include countries in South America, West and East Africa, South East Asia and several Pacific Ocean island groups. The three most useful sources of information on timber utilisation in these countries are the publications of UNIDO (UN Industrial and Development Organisation), ITTO (International Tropical Timber Organisation) and IUFRO (International Union of Forestry Research Organisations). There is also useful information to be found in the proceeding of the CIB-W18B Conferences on Tropical and Hardwood Timber Construction in Singapore in 1987 and in Kuala Lumpur, Malaysia in 1992.

There are many features of the timber, climate and infrastructure of these countries which conspire to make it difficult or inappropriate to apply North American technology (Leicester 1988a, 1988b). For example the often stated specification that the test environment be at approximately 23°C may necessitate that laboratories in tropical countries be airconditioned, an expensive and often unaffordable restriction, and one that is totally unnecessary in many instances.

The first difficulty in utilisation to be noted in these countries arises from the fact that there are several thousand species of trees growing in their forests. Hence it is not feasible to undertake in-grade testing on a species by species basis as is done in North America. So far, the only structural classification procedures applied imply a necessity for species identification; species are grouped into structural classes on the basis of clear wood properties and their design rules are related to these classes (Leicester and Keating 1982). One of the few attempts to examine the possibility of stress-grading mixtures of unidentified species is a Malaysian investigation into the use of mechanical stress grading (Collins and Ashaari Hj. Mohd Amin 1990).

The second difficulty relates to the development of technology for construction with unseasoned hardwoods in a tropical environment. Perhaps Australian experience may be useful here (Dept. of Works and Housing 1946).

Finally there are problems related to the limited technology infrastructure of many tropical countries. Although most of these countries have excellent research facilities, frequently there are deficiencies in the production and quality control of structural material, in the supply of suitable structural material, in the standard of building construction, in the relevant building regulations and in the technical information available to designers. All these factors discourage the use of structural timber for indigenous construction.

Perhaps one solution would be to draft and implement simplified versions of the North American type of design codes, material standards and building regulations. Effectively this would lead to simplicity at the expense of efficiency. However the loss of efficiency would be of little practical consequence as tropical timbers are frequently 2-4 times as strong as North American softwoods. The benefit would be the rapid utilisation of lesser known species.

An alternative approach to utilisation would be to select only one or two favoured species for indigenous construction. Such an approach has been used successfully by some engineers/architects in Malaysia.

Globalization

At a significant NATO Advanced Research Workshop on the topic of Reliability-Based Design of Engineered Wood Structures held in Firenze, Italy in 1991, an emphatic conclusion reached by the academics and researchers present was that the most urgent task for timber engineering technologists is the globalisation of timber as a structural material. Currently it is possible for a structural engineer trained in the design of steel structures to undertake such designs in almost any country in the world with a minimum of special information. However this is not so for timber structures. Each region or country has its own special group of species, its own classification procedures, its own quality control and regulatory control system and its own design code. As a result, structural timber may be considered as a local material, often suitable only for use in "cottage" construction. Until structural timber technology is globalised, it will not be a subject of major academic concern; until structural timber technology is globalised, there will always be difficulties in technology transfer between countries and in the trade of structural products.

An obvious course of action would be to rely on the use of ISO codes and standards. There are two potential drawbacks to this action. First it is likely that it will probably be a long time before there is available a comprehensive set of ISO standards; there will also be long delays in modifying those standards as difficulties arise during their application. The second negative aspect of relying on ISO standards is that unless they have the right format, they will merely legitimise the standards of one particular region and create difficulties and disadvantages for others.

The following are three sets of considerations that must be included in any plan for globalisation. First, because of the expense and time that has already been incurred in classifying materials according to current national and regional standards, it is necessary to harmonise these standards. In this context the term "harmonisation" is taken to refer to establishing an equivalence between two performance standards; an example of this relative to in-grade evaluation of structural timber properties has been given in previous papers (Leicester et al 1996a and 1996b). The importance of such work can be gauged from the fact that it costs roughly a million US dollars and the resources for one year of a fully equipped laboratory to undertake the detailed in-grade evaluation of a single species according to the performance standard of a single country.

The second requirement for ISO standards to be globally effective is that they should be applicable to any country, timber resource, climate, and building system.

Much of the research in North America and Europe, such as that on load duration effects, is often reported in terms of the timber strength. However as this research has been undertaken only on a limited range of softwood species, and the strength of timbers utilised internationally often falls well outside this range, the research would be more globally applicable if it were to be reported in terms of factors that are not species dependant. For example, if the structural behaviour depends on the magnitude of natural defects, then a definition of grade quality such as the following would be more suitable than timber strength;

$$\text{grade quality} = \frac{\text{mean clear wood strength}}{5\text{-percentile in-grade bending strength}}$$

Another example of restrictive technology relates to the specification of size effects. The appropriate exponent for describing the effect of size on the bending strength of sawn lumber has been the subject of considerable discussion among North American and European research groups. However size effects are not globally applicable. Among other factors they depend on timber species, log sizes, sawing patterns and grading methods. In fact it is possible, as has been noted in some Australian timber resources, that measured size effects may turn out to be described by negative exponents. It would restrict the applicability of an ISO standard if it required the same size effect for all sawn timber.

Finally, for reasons given in the preceding section on tropical countries, ISO codes and standards should be sufficiently flexible that a particular country or region would be able to trade off efficiency in material utilisation in order to operate with design simplicity and reduced quality control costs. One method to achieve this would be to draft tiered ISO codes and standards, each tier being associated with its own level of efficiency and simplicity. It is anticipated that this topic will be discussed at a forthcoming meeting of the APEC Subcommittee on Standards and Conformance.

Conclusions

The review of research trends around the world has indicated many similarities and a few differences to the research on timber engineering currently being undertaken in North America. The countries and regions reviewed were Europe, Australasia, Japan, South Africa and tropical countries in general.

Fundamental research incudes research related to mechano-sorptive effects, wood-steel composite construction, stress-grading, fire resistance and joints for connecting large elements, particularly the aspect of their resistance against earthquake loading.

An increasing driver of research is the need to develop performance criteria, not only for design but also for technology transfer and for trade purposes. Important topics here include methods for assessing the dynamic characteristics of floor systems and methods for assessing the strength under long duration loads of wood-based materials and of glued joints. There is also a related need to develop probabilistic models for predicting biodegradation effects.

Finally there is research driven by the desire to globalise timber engineering. This requires the development of performance criteria that may be used to harmonise the national standards of various countries and regions, and also the development of technology required for drafting globally applicable ISO standards. Global standards should be based on technology that is equally applicable to all structural timber material; they also should be useable in all countries, whether highly developed or with a limited technology infrastructure.

References

Appleton, R.G. (1993). A Research Project on Timber Frame Construction for Apartment (BCA Class 2) Buildings up to Three Storeys in Height. National Assoc. of Forest Industries, Canberra, Australia. 300pp.

Blass, H.J. (1996). Timber Engineering Education in Europe. Proc. of International Wood Engineering Conference. New Orleans, USA. Oct. Vol.3, pp.11-14.

Collins, M.J., Ashaari Hj. Mohd Amin (1990). Investigation of Machine Grading of Malaysian Tropical Hardwoods. Proc. of 1990 International Timber Engineering Conference. Tokyo, Japan. Oct. Vol.3, pp.827-833.

Crews, K. and Walter, G. (1996). Five Years of Stress Laminated Timber Bridges in Australia - A Review of Development and Application. Proc. of International Wood Engineering Conference. New Orleans, USA. Vol.1, pp.221-229.

Department of Works and Housing (1946). A Report on the Structural Soundness of Unseasoned Timbers Used in Structures Erected for Wartime Purposes. Melbourne, Australia.

Ellingwood, B., Galambos, T.V., McGregor, J.G. and Cornell, C.A. (1980). Development of a Probability Based Load Criterion for American National Standard A58. NBS Special Pub. No. 577, US Dept. of Commerce, Washington D.C., USA.

Enjily, V. and Mettam, C.J. (1995). Medium-Rise Timber Frame Buildings. Feasibility Study. TRADA and DOE, UK.

Leicester, R.H. (1988a). Challenges to Research in Wood Engineering: South-East Asian/Australasian Point of View. Proc. of International Conference on Timber Engineering. Seattle, USA. Sept. Vol.1, pp.60-64.

Leicester, R.H. (1988b). Timber Engineering Standards for Tropical Countries. Proc. of International Conference on Timber Engineering. Seattle, USA. Sept. Vol.1, pp.177-185.

Leicester, R.H. (1994). Statistical Control of Stress Graded Lumber. Proc. of Statistical Process Technologies: State of the Art for the Forest Products Industry. Portland, USA. Nov. pp.63-70.

Leicester, R.H. (1995). Fire Codes and Timber Structures in Australia. Proc. of National Workshop on Fire and Timber in Modern Building Design. Kuala Lumpur, Malaysia. July. pp.14-28.

Leicester, R.H. (1996). A Reliability Model for Durability. Proc. of 25th Forest Products Research Conference, paper 2/14. Melbourne, Australia. Nov. Vol.1.

Leicester, R.H., Breitinger, H.O. and Fordham, H. (1996a). Equivalence of In-grade Testing Standards. Proc. of CIB-W18 Meeting 29, Paper No. 29-6-20, Bordeaux, France, August.

Leicester, R.H., Breitinger, H.O. and Fordham, H. (1996b). Proc. of International Wood Engineering Conference. New Orleans, USA. Oct. Vol.2, pp.271-276.

Leicester, R.H. and Craig, C.A. (1996). Application of Microwave Scanners for Stress Grading. Proc. of International Wood Engineering Conference. New Orleans, USA. Oct. Vol.2, pp.435-442.

Leicester, R.H. and Keating, W.G. (1982). Use of Strength Classifications for Timber Engineering Standards. Division of Building Research Tech. Paper (Second Series) No. 43. CSIRO, Melbourne, Australia.

Leicester, R.H., Pham, L., Holmes, J.D. and Bridge, R.O. (1986). Proc. of Seminar on Safety of Limit-States Structural Design Codes. Institution of Engineers, Australia. Melbourne, Australia, March.

McKenzie, C. (1996). A Reliability Based Durability Design Method for Timber: An Overview. Proc. Of 25th Forest Products Research Conference, Paper 2/1. Melbourne, Australia. Nov. Vol.1.

Mettam, C.J., Pitts, G.C., Steer, P.J. and Enjily, V. (1996). Current Developments in Medium-Rise Timber Frame Buildings in the UK. Paper 25-15-4. Proc. of 29th Meeting of CIB-W18. Bordeaux, France. August.

Reardon, G.F. and Henderson, D. (1996). Simulates Wind Loading on a Two Storey Test House. Proc. of International Wood Engineering Conference. New Orleans, USA. Oct. Vol.4, pp.313-327.

Standards Australia (1978). AS1748. Mechanically stress-graded timber. Sydney, Australia.

Standards Australia (1979). Visually stress-graded Hardwood for Structural Purposes. Sydney, Australia.

Standards Australia (1986a). AS:2878. Timber-classification into strength groups. Sydney, Australia.

Standards Australia (1986b) AS 2858. Timber-softwood-visually Stress-graded for Structural Purposes. Sydney, Australia.

Standards Australia/Standards New Zealand. (1992 AS/NZS:4063. Timber-Stress-graded-In-grade strength and stiffness evaluation. Sydney, Australia.

Standards Australia (1993). AS3519 Timber-machine Proof Grading. Sydney, Australia.

Vinopal, G.W. (1985). Grading and Testing Machines Developed at NTRI, CSIR. Proc. Of Forest Products Research International-Achievements and the Future. Paper 3/16 Pretoria, South Africa. April. Vol.4.

New Directions in Wood Engineering

David S. Gromala[1], Member, ASCE

Abstract

Rather than attempting to predict grand changes in wood engineering during the next 10 to 20 years, this paper predicts the potential impacts of several trends that are already underway. The trends of combining wood and nonwood materials, of updating product standards to performance-bases, and of the accelerating pace of information are explored. These trends are examined separately, and are also presented against the backdrop of the continuing changes in our wood resource. Specific research needs in each of these areas are presented with the hope that each of these trends will have positive, rather than negative, impacts on wood engineering in the 21st century.

Introduction

It's not easy to write a paper entitled "New Directions in Wood Engineering" for a workshop entitled "Wood Engineering in the 21st Century." I stumbled from an attempt at a "psychic" draft (trying to envision this field in 10 to 20 years) to a "state-of-the-art" draft. Neither draft fit the goal of a "position paper" -- where the purpose is to provide a personal viewpoint on the broad and futuristic topic of where we are, or might be, headed in the next decade. With this goal as a roadmap, this paper began to emerge. Although my crystal ball can see dozens of topics to discuss in this paper, I'll focus on three areas that have the biggest potential impacts on wood engineering.

Trend 1. We will see increasing combination of wood with other materials in structural products.

Trend 2. We can expect virtually universal acceptance of performance-based standards as a basis for design values.

---

[1]Senior Engineering Specialist, Weyerhaeuser, Technology Center, Tacoma, WA 98477

Trend 3. We should prepare for continued acceleration of the pace of information availability and engineering sophistication.

I believe that our success in managing these trends, which are all currently gaining momentum, will largely determine our success or failure as a major player in the structural materials industry. This is not to say that other macro-issues will not play a role in the future. The cycles in national and world economies will continue, environmental issues will evolve further, and the speed and availability of information will continue its dizzying pace. However, this is not a paper on economic modeling, political prognostication, or the curses of information overload -- it's a paper on new directions in wood engineering.

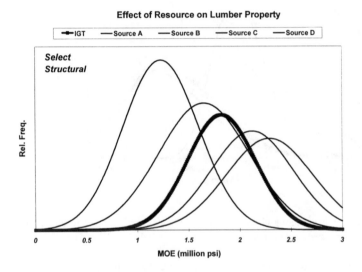

Figure 1. Lumber that meets visual grade requirements from a specific resource can be *somewhat stiffer or significantly less stiff* than in-grade test (IGT) data.

Overriding Issue: The Changing Resource

There is one macro-issue that not only impacts all three topic areas, but will likely govern our future handling of all structural wood products. That issue is our **changing resource**. The changing resource is a snowball coming down the mountain. It's a little further away in some regions than in others, but it's still on its way. This issue is alarming in two respects -- first, because many in our industry appear to be ignoring it; and second, because our existing product standards don't have the tools to cope with it.

While the speed of these changes is differential by region, users will see increasing amounts of wood fiber coming from smaller diameter and/or faster grown trees. What are the implications of this inevitable shift? Wood-based products will contain more juvenile wood in the future than in the past. Juvenile wood is generally less dense than mature wood and exhibits more significant dimensional changes under moisture cycling. It can also be less stiff and strong than mature wood (see figures 1 and 2).

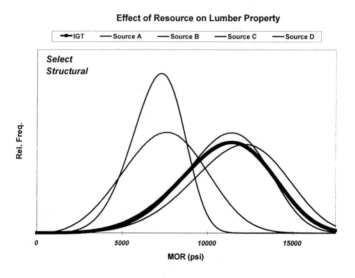

Figure 2. Lumber meeting visual grade requirements from a specific resource can be *somewhat stronger or significantly weaker* than in-grade test (IGT) data.

The wood products industry must address these issues before they reach a critical stage. To address dimensional stability, manufacturers must implement improved drying techniques or develop high-tech stabilization methods to continue to serve those markets that require dimensionally stable material. To address structural properties, product standards must be updated to acknowledge that current predictors of strength and stiffness properties may be inadequate to characterize this new material. The standards must be performance-based, but they must also be incentive-based -- giving proper credit to producers who continuously monitor their structural properties relative to those who don't. Such advances in product standards would lead to the increasing implementation of new technologies for product sorting and grading.

With this as a backdrop, let's proceed into a discussion of the three focal areas, presenting visions of the success factors and potential warning signs for each, and discussing how the rapidly changing resource must be accommodated to succeed in each.

Trend 1. Increasing combination of wood with other materials in structural products

Wood and Reinforcing Fibers. Fiber-reinforcing of glulam beams on a commercial basis has emerged during the past decade. Improvements in this technology and its expansion to other product lines offers the potential to produce wood-based structural products with properties formerly unattainable.   The dynamics of wood/fiber prices and of fiber/adhesive technologies promise advances that could fundamentally change the high-performance structural member market. Progress in this area will hinge on continued development of sound theoretical bases for analysis and design, proper consideration of bonding and durability issues, proper manufacturing controls, and continual monitoring of product performance.

Note that fiber-reinforcing need not be limited to aramid, carbon and glass fibers. Advances in polymer-cellulose technology and other cellulose modification technologies may prove to be superior alternatives over the long run. For example, a commercially available polymer-enhanced cellulosic sheet, has already found applications in reinforcing of sheet products, and could be expected to fit well into other applications. Finally, the low cost per unit stiffness of steel reinforcing continues to lead researchers to search for ways to produce wood-steel composites.

Broader combination of materials. Combination of materials may progress into areas other than fiber reinforcing of wood. Wood fiber in some form may be used in combination with light gauge steel sections to prevent premature buckling of the steel sections. New, ductile ceramic materials may prove to have properties that are very compatible with wood. New types of adhesives might lead to gluelines that actually contain the reinforcing materials. Some of the thousands of new polymer materials will likely exhibit properties that uniquely complement wood in composite structural applications. Advances in microelectronics will eventually lead to the embedment of sensors into structural members that will measure in-place stress levels with the members.

Just as some reinforcing materials will give wood-based members higher strength and stiffness, special production techniques or chemical stabilizers will give them better dimensional stability. For example, commercially available OSB with enhanced edge-treatments and laminated-strand lumber products exhibit significantly better dimensional stability than their competitors. Should we ever achieve that "holy grail" of the completely dimensionally stable wood product, we can penetrate market niches currently unavailable to wood. For example, such a product could utilize new connection technologies that would be freed from the need to accommodate wood's shrinkage and swelling.

The combination of wood and other materials will lead to new markets and expanded opportunities for engineered wood products. Successful products will use sound engineering analysis methods in product analysis and design, based on a fundamental understanding of the short- and long-term performance of these products, and incorporating appropriate quality control techniques in the manufacturing process. Potential warning signs will appear when product developers attempt to "piggyback" on the least-stringent provisions in other wood products standards, do not understand their product's engineering characteristics, or over-economize on QC and followup testing.

Impact of the changing resource on these new materials

Innovative products often receive code and market acceptance based on significant structural testing during the initial product development phase, followed by only minimal continued verification testing once commercial production begins. This poses two problems when the wood portion of the product comes from a changing resource.

The first problem arises if the initial development testing did not fully characterize the wood used in that testing. Significant errors can be introduced during this stage if, for example, the wood is assumed to have "handbook" strength and stiffness values. Additional errors, primarily due to lack of complete engineering information, arise if the new product's performance is characterized on a statistical basis rather than on an engineering stress analysis basis.

The second problem caused by a changing resource in this scenario arises when the material coming into the manufacturing plant differs from that used in the qualification testing. The differences that might lead to final product failures can be as subtle as changes in the dimensional stability or gluability of the wood or as dramatic as major shifts in the wood's strength or stiffness due to changes in the incoming resource.

The recommendation here is obvious -- developers of structural products made from a combination of wood and other materials must assume the responsibility for fully characterizing the *specific* properties of the *specific* materials (both wood and nonwood) used in their development phases, they must develop their design capacities based on engineering stress analysis that quantifies the impact of changes in incoming material properties, and they must implement rigorous quality control procedures in their manufacturing process to prove that the structural performance of daily production meets qualification levels.

Specific Research Needs

1. Fundamental study of bonding mechanisms and bond durability between solid wood and other materials.

2. Consolidation of knowledge related to failure theories for wood products, and expansion of those theories to reinforced members.

3. Advancements in product standards and design specifications that

establish structural performance requirements for highly consistent (i.e., low COV) products -- at performance levels that are compatible with historical engineering judgement not only for wood products, but for nonwood products (e.g., steel, composites, etc.).

4. Fundamental research into wood stabilization.

Trend 2. Total acceptance of performance-based standards as a basis for design values

As building code provisions continue to evolve in North America, one of the often-stated objectives is to increase the acceptance of performance-based standards (as opposed to prescriptive standards) as the basis for product acceptance and use recommendations. When properly conceived and implemented, performance-based standards permit new products to maximize their engineering potential, thus accelerating their market penetration.

Recent advances in wood-based product standards have led to performance-based grading of structural panel products, and to rapid growth in the availability of prefabricated I-joists and structural composite lumber products. The success of these products is, in part, due to the development of consensus-based standards for each product that establish basic engineering methodologies, qualification requirements and quality control recommendations that are appropriate for that product. Potential warning signs in this area have arisen when new products choose to borrow standards provisions from other product lines or to utilize nonstandardized techniques for evaluating engineering adequacy -- as illustrated in the following examples.

Limited Empirical Testing. One example of borrowing standards provisions from other product lines relates to fabricated structural products adopting empirical qualification testing in lieu of engineering stress analysis. For example, a new fabricated product may select portions of existing standards for sawn lumber, and conclude that flexural design values can be based solely on an estimate of the near-minimum property (e.g., a fifth-percentile estimate) divided by a specific reduction factor (e.g., 2.1). This limited information can be misapplied by testing as few as 28 pieces of a new product, dividing the lowest test value by 2.1, and assigning the design value (forever and ever) on that basis.

This approach ignores the fact that the sawn lumber standards require broad geographic sampling to ensure representativeness, that they are based on additional conservative assumptions related to grade and size modeling, that they result in very high average safety factors for typical lumber production, and that they apply to lumber in widths and lengths that are primarily used in structurally redundant applications.

In a worst case scenario, the 28 tests on the fabricated product have extremely low variability (for that lot), are accepted by the codes and by the market, and are applied to a product with very long span capability made from input materials whose properties vary from lot to lot. Unless the qualification tests are supplemented by a rigorous daily quality control program, there is no "safety net" in this process. Unfortunately, this scenario can lead to products that (at best) compromise safety level, or (at worst) fail in service.

Nonstandardized Reliability Analysis. In the mid-1990s, we are working our way through a "learning curve" that will teach us how to best use reliability-based analysis in the future. The power of this new technology is enormous. Unfortunately, the limitations of this technology are equally enormous. During the past decade, we progressed from the naive notion that the reliability index was a true measure of failure probability to the more accurate viewpoint that it is a relative measure. We developed standards that acknowledge the need for standardized analysis assumptions and numerical techniques prior to acceptance of reliability-based results in structural applications.

The potential dangers of reliability-based analysis during this interim period are in the possible code-acceptance of a product based on product-specific reliability calculations rather than on compliance with the existing framework of product standards. Such calculations provide results that are highly dependent on a host of assumptions and, if applied for competitive advantage, would present a highly unstable basis for new product acceptance.

The ASTM committee that developed D5457-93 in the U.S. were so concerned by the instability of results obtained by nonstandardized reliability analyses that they limited its use to the development of "normalization factors" computed under a strict set of reference analysis conditions. Note that the problems related to product-specific reliability analysis become magnified as additional parameters are added into the analysis. For example, reliability analysis of a product destined for use as a beam can involve the relatively straightforward comparison of the distribution of flexural capacities to an assumed distribution of floor or roof loads. However, if that product is to be used as a floor joist, the analysis could also include the complexities of floor system analysis and even of alternative limit states -- neither of which has any consensus-standards basis.

Impact of the changing resource on performance-based standards

The lesson here is similar to that discussed for new wood/nonwood composites. Performance-based standards must be established with the understanding that the wood resource is changing. They must account for fluctuations in properties due to differences in material sources (i.e., purchasing faster-grown trees this week and long-rotation trees the next). They must also account for longer term trends in resource availability (i.e., as the predominant species in a given species group gradually changes over time). And, as before, they must provide credit for producers who continuously monitor their structural properties.

Specific Research Needs

    1. Development of statistically justified methods by which the accuracy of structural property assignment can be measured and design benefits can be quantified. (Galligan and Green, in their 1983 workshop position paper, stated that "The challenge, however, is to identify a reward for accuracy in property assignment beyond that of MSR. This is a subject not clearly understood by most researchers.")

    2. Incorporation of standardized load and resistance distributions and reliability analysis procedures into consensus-based standards to form the basis for design value assignment based on reliability principles.

    3. Establishment of recommended procedures for analysis of complex systems (or, at a minimum, of recommended reporting criteria to enable proper peer evaluation of the analysis results) and establishment of target safety levels for assemblies.

    4. Establishment of recommended procedures for generating design adjustment factors destined for broad use (e.g., enhanced repetitive member factors that could be used in floors, walls and roofs of any conceivable configuration should not be based solely on simple span, uniform load analyses).

Trend 3. Accelerating pace of information availability and engineering sophistication

Some of the trends that are leading us into the 21st century are obvious. Unbelievable advances in microelectronics will continue to provide us with easier and cheaper access to information of all kinds. Rapid increases in the number of people with access to the Internet will make that information available to virtually everyone. For design engineers, access to increasingly sophisticated design software will permit them to squeeze more and more inefficiencies out of their designs. Researchers, like designers, will have access to new generations of software tools, ever-expanding sources of input data for their modeling ventures, and easy access to potential research-users via the Internet.

While it has never been documented, it is likely that users of the earliest mechanical counting equipment (like the abacus) knew that skill and care were required in choosing the correct numbers to begin a calculation if there would be any hope that the final result of the numerical manipulation would be correct. In other words, the concept behind the term GIGO ("Garbage In, Garbage Out") almost certainly precedes modern computational equipment.

Unfortunately, several factors are working against us in our battle to **maximize output data** and to **minimize output garbage**: 1) computational equipment can produce more numbers than we can ever hope to check for accuracy; 2) many organizations are attempting to accomplish more work with fewer people; 3) overall information overload bombards us into numbness -- decreasing our intuitive "feel" for which information is correct and which is bogus, 4) technological progress leads to increased specialization and narrower focus (i.e., more computational power leads users to employ more complex models; more complex models require more sophisticated inputs, more sophisticated inputs require even narrower technological study, etc, etc).

Discussion of Increasing Engineering "Sophistication". When one attempts to solve an engineering problem, one starts with a definition of the problem (a "model") and some sense of the desired outputs. The actual "engineering" process consists of developing an understanding of the mechanisms at work and determining how to best model those mechanisms numerically. Various engineers and researchers spend varying amounts of time thinking about two equally important "details" -- the input data needed to "drive" the model and the test results needed to verify the results of the model.

In the "old days" of master architects and engineer/contractors, one person was responsible for all phases of engineering modeling. When the engineer was required to stand under his bridge while a fully-loaded train crossed it, he became intimately familiar with all of these aspects -- one way or another.

As we progress into increasingly specialized areas of expertise, we are losing that familiarity with all of the ingredients of successful engineering. Those who work full-time modeling (or, for designers, crunching designs) are forced to trust that their material property inputs -- provided by other specialists working full-time in property-development -- produce acceptable outputs. And it is rare that any of these specialists has the luxury of actually observing the construction of the buildings that they model or design.

As we reach the end of this millennium, this system has the potential of breaking down even further due to accelerating information availability. Material characterizations are becoming more exotic. Design standards are becoming more complex. Code requirements are increasingly based on the latest research study rather than on the sum total of our collective engineering judgement and experience.

One prescription to improve this situation in the next millennium is to :

> 1. Commit to broaden our individual and collective experience base -- to develop an intuitive "feel" for what works and what doesn't.

> 2. Update our codes and standards on an evolutionary rather than a revolutionary basis -- trusting our profession's collective judgment and experience to lead us, and using "rocket science" modeling to refine, rather than redefine, these judgments.

3. Know our limitations. Know our model's limitations -- and publicize them! For example, when a model is developed for a specific application and is tested over a limited range of conditions, clearly state those limitations and perform "reality checks," asking what would happen to the model results if something didn't happen quite as precisely as it was modeled --if the material properties were different than those assumed, if the product were installed differently than assumed, if the physical uses were different than those assumed -- would the product still perform? At what level? Would it lead to a catastrophic failure?

Impact of the changing resource on accelerating engineering complexity

In today's system, engineers are rewarded for designing a product to span further than before. Researchers are rewarded for developing bigger adjustment factors than before. While we will still look to engineers and researchers for these advancements in the future, we will ask them to add two new hurdles to their analyses -- to *prove* that their calculations are correct first, for a broad range of material property values and second, across the whole range of anticipated structural use configurations.

Specific Research Needs

1. Establish regular "exchange programs" in which academic or government researchers spend time in design offices and at active jobsites.

2. Develop Internet-based discussion groups to debate wood engineering issues (e.g., software testing anomalies, analysis techniques, field experiences with various products, etc).

3. Develop Internet-based "standard design configurations" or "standard data sets" for use as reference points by model developers.

Summary

A host of challenges await us as we proceed toward the 21st century. Wood-based structural products will be pushed by market forces and by technical advances. Materials technologies will continue to remove traditional boundaries between materials. Successful new products will routinely include innovative combinations of materials. New generations of standards will be available that permit rapid introduction of these innovative products into the market. Information technologies in many forms will ease our ability to develop these products, analyze their performance, design their applications, and even advertise their benefits. The 21st century will challenge us to advance at this fast pace without losing sight of our fundamentals -- engineering judgment, breadth of applications experience, and an ever-present focus on our underlying assumptions and limitations.

OTHER WORKSHOP INFORMATION

Wood Structures Tour

Kevin Cheung, M. ASCE and Erik Wilson

The Wood Structures Tour provided interested workshop participants an opportunity to visit two wood structures under construction in Portland, Oregon. The tour was organized and conducted by Kevin Cheung and Erik Wilson of Western Wood Products Association, Ned Adamson of Kramer Gehlen & Associates and Paul Gilham of Western Wood Structures. The two projects are (1) Pearl Court Apartments — a four- and five-story multi-family residential wood frame construction, and (2) Potash Facility — a 230,000 sq. ft single level curved-Glulam arch structure.

Pearl Court Apartment
Project Engineer: Rehan Jaddi of KPFF Consulting Engineers, Portland, Oregon

The City of Portland recently approved five-story wood-frame construction within city limits and along transit corridors to reduce urban sprawls and to provide affordable housing. The Pearl Court Apartment is Portland's first five-story wood-frame project. The building occupies one entire street block consisting of four- and five-story wood frame structures. The walls are framed with Douglas Fir-Larch and Hem Fir solid-sawn lumber, with S-Dry material for studs

Photo by Ned Adamson

and MC 15 material for wall plates and sills. The roof system is metal-plate-connected wood trusses. The floor and ceiling joists are Douglas Fir-Larch lumber joists and wood I-joists. Designing to UBC Seismic Zone III required the use of shearwalls and tie-downs at wall ends. Standard details are used otherwise.

Potash Facility
Project Engineer: Paul Gilham, Western Wood Structures, Inc., Tualatin, Oregon

The Potash Facility project is a 230,000 square feet single level potash storage and loading facility located in North Portland on the Columbia River. A reclaimer standing 60 feet tall and 150 feet wide moves lengthwise through the structure.

Actual dimensions are 160 feet wide pin-to-pin and 85 feet floor-to-crown. Due to the corrosive nature of potash to steel, Glulam was selected for the structural system. The Glulam members are Willamette Industries' 115

Photo by Ned Adamson

feet long 24FV8 with an 8-3/4" by 55-1/2" cross section. Transportation of the Glulam members to the job site required special consideration. The metal connectors are not galvanized but are protected with three layers of paint. The structure is designed for 90 mph wind speed, 25 psf snow load and UBC Seismic Zone III. The design for lateral forces is governed by wind in most cases.

List of Participants

Beckry Abdel-Magid	Winona State University
D. G. Barreira	Lockheed Martin
Frank Beall	University of California
Christine Beaulieu	Trus Joist MacMillan
Don Bender*	Washington State University
Robert Brooks	Willamette Industries, Inc.
William Bulleit*	Michigan Technological University
Michael Caldwell	American Institute of Timber Construction
Ray Chalfant	Jr. Consulting Engineer
Mark Chang	LateralPro Technology
Kevin Cheung*	Western Wood Products Association
Peggy Clouston	University of British Columbia
Steven Cramer*	Weyerhaeuser
Marvin Criswell	Colorado State University
Thomas Cunningham, Jr.	J.M. Huber Corporation
Habib Dagher*	University of Maine
Nirmal Das	Georgia Southern University
Donald DeVisser	West Coast Lumber Inspection Bureau
James Dolan*	Virginia Tech
Sheila Rimal Duwadi	U.S. Department of Transportation
Caroline Frenette	The University of British Columbia
Kenneth Fridley	Washington State University
Vijaya Gopu	Louisiana State University
Kiril Gramatikov	Shopje, Macedonia
David Gromala	Weyerhaeuser
Rakesh Gupta*	Oregon State University
Bert Hall	H.E. Bergeron Civil Engr.
Robert Hendershot	R2H Engineering, Inc.
Mark Henderson	Lockwood Jones and Beals, Inc.
Bruce Hess	Trus Joist MacMillan
Paula Hilbrich Lee	USDA - Forest Service
Jean-Francois Houde	Canadian Wood Council
Lin Hu	Forintek Canada Corp.
Dominique Janssens*	Structural Board Association
Lisa Johnson	Southern Pine Inspection Bureau
Kenneth Johnson	Wheeler Consolidated, Inc.
Fumio Kamiya	Forestry and Forest Products Research Institute
Gerald Kammerman	Washington County, Oregon
John Kampmann, Jr.	MEA Engineers, Inc.
Meho Karalic	Matrix Timber Ltd

149

Stephen Kent	FR3
John Kerns	Weyerhaeuser
Jai Kim	Bucknell University
David Kretschman	USDA - Forest Service
George Kyanka	State University of New York
Edward Laatsch	State Farm Insurance Comapnies
Peter Lau	Forintek Canada Corp.
Robert Leichti*	Oregon State University
Philip Line	American Forest & Paper Association
Borg Madsen	Timber Engineering Ltd
John Maly	Trus Joist MacMillan
Harvey Manbeck	Penn State University
Catherine Marx	Southern Forest Products Association
Thomas McLain	Oregon State University
Daniel McNaughton	Daniel McNaughton & Associates
Christopher Meyer	Trus Joist MacMillan
Russ Moody	USDA - Forest Service
David Moses	The University of British Columbia
Brad Nelson	Trus Joist MacMillan
Sherman Nelson	Consulting Engineer
Paul Nicholas	Trus Joist MacMillan
Michael O'Halloran	APA - The Engineered Wood Assoc.
Marcia Patton-Mallory	US Forest Service
Phillip Pierce	McFarland-Johnson, Inc.
David Pollock	Washington State University
Robert Reitherman	CUREe
Adam Rolin	A.G. Rolin Consulting
David Rosowsky*	Clemson University
Scott Schiff	Clemson University
Richard Schmidt*	University of Wyoming
Don Sharp	Trus Joist MacMillan
Bradley Shelley	West Coast Lumber Inspection Bureau
John Silva	Hilti Corp.
Thomas Skaggs	APA
David Soderquist	Willamette Industries, Inc.
Stanley Suddarth	Purdue University
Ed Sutton	National Association of Home Builders
Steven Taylor	Trus Joist MacMillan
Robert Tichy*	Washington State University
Dan Tingley	Wood Science and Technology Institute, Inc.
Charles Transue	Willbros Engineers, Inc.
Michael Triche*	The University of Alabama
Miles Waltz	Oregon State University
Jason Weber	Sampson Engineering, Inc.
Dan Werdowatz	Josephson Werdowatz & Associates
Gary Williams	Timber Systems Limited
Thomas Williamson	Engineered Wood Systems
Ron Wolfe	U.S. Forest Products Laboratory
Borjen Yeh	APA - The Engineered Wood Assoc.

*Group facilitator

Workshop Groups

Group 1 Facilitator: Members:	Don Bender, Washington State University John Kampmann, Jr., MEA Engineers, Inc. Paul Nicholas, Trus Joist MacMillan Thomas Skaggs, APA Thomas Williamson, Engineered Wood Systems
Group 2 Facilitator: Members:	Dominique Janssens, Structural Board Association Mark Chang, LateralPro Technology Caroline Frenette, The University of British Columbia Fumio Kamiya, Forestry & Forest Products Research Institute John Silva, Hilti Corp. Gary Williams, Timber Systems Limited
Group 3 Facilitator: Members:	James Dolan, Virginia Tech Christine Beaulieu, Trus Joist MacMillan Peggy Clouston, University of British Columbia David Gromala, Weyerhaeuser Meho Karalic, Matrix Timber Ltd Michael O'Halloran, APA - The Engineered Wood Assoc. Adam Rolin, A.G. Rolin Consulting Scott Schiff, Clemson University Jason Weber, Sampson Engineering, Inc. Ron Wolfe, U.S. Forest Products Laboratory
Group 4 Facilitator: Members:	Kevin Cheung, Western Wood Products Association Donald DeVisser, West Coast Lumber Inspection Bureau Lisa Johnson, Southern Pine Inspection Bureau Philip Line, American Forest & Paper Association John Maly, Trus Joist MacMillan Thomas McLain, Oregon State University David Pollock, Washington State University
Group 5 Facilitator: Members:	William Bulleit, Michigan Technological University Robert Hendershot, R2H Engineering, Inc. Kenneth Johnson, Wheeler Consolidated, Inc. Edward Laatsch, State Farm Insurance Comapnies Steven Taylor, Trus Joist MacMillan Dan Tingley, Wood Science and Technology Institute

Group 6 Facilitator: Steven Cramer, Weyerhaeuser
Members: Michael Caldwell, American Institute of Timber Construction
                       Sheila Rimal Duwadi, U.S. Department of Transportation
                       Bert Hall, H.E. Bergeron Civil Engr.
                       Mark Henderson, Lockwood, Jones and Beals, Inc.

Group 7 Facilitator: Rakesh Gupta, Oregon State University
Members: Beckry Abdel-Magid, Winona State University
                       Ray Chalfant, Jr., Consulting Engineer
                       Gerald Kammerman, Washington County, Oregon
                       Bradley Shelley, West Coast Lumber Inspection Bureau
                       Charles Transue, Willbros Engineers, Inc.

Group 8 Facilitator: Michael Triche, The University of Alabama
Members: D. G. Barreira, Lockheed Martin
                       John Kerns, Weyerhaeuser
                       Jai Kim, Bucknell University
                       Russ Moody, USDA - Forest Service
                       David Moses, The University of British Columbia
                       Brad Nelson, Trus Joist MacMillan
                       Stanley Suddarth, Purdue University

Group 9 Facilitator: Robert Tichy, Washington State University
Members: Frank Beall, University of California
                       David Kretschman, USDA - Forest Service
                       Marcia Patton-Mallory, US Forest Service
                       Robert Reitherman, CUREe
                       Borjen Yeh, APA - The Engineered Wood Assoc.

Group 10 Facilitator: Habib Dagher, University of Maine
Members: Robert Brooks, Willamette Industries, Inc.
                       Kiril Gramatikov, Shopje, Macedonia
                       Paula Hilbrich Lee, USDA - Forest Service
                       Harvey Manbeck, Penn State University
                       Sherman Nelson, Consulting Engineer
                       Ed Sutton, National Association of Home Builders

Group 11 Facilitator: Richard Schmidt, University of Wyoming
Members: Marvin Criswell, Colorado State University
                       Thomas Cunningham, Jr., J.M. Huber Corporation
                       Jean-Francois Houde, Canadian Wood Council
                       Lin Hu, Forintek Canada Corp.
                       Stephen Kent, FR3
                       George Kyanka, State University of New York
                       Christopher Meyer, Trus Joist MacMillan

Group 12 Facilitator: Robert Leichti, Oregon State University
Members: Nirmal Das, Georgia Southern University
Peter Lau, Forintek Canada Corp.
Phillip Pierce, McFarland-Johnson, Inc.
David Soderquist, Willamette Industries, Inc.
Miles Waltz, Oregon State University

Group 13 Facilitator: David Rosowsky, Clemson University
Members: Bruce Hess, Trus Joist MacMillan
Borg Madsen, Timber Engineering Ltd
Daniel McNaughton, Daniel McNaughton & Associates
Don Sharp, Trus Joist MacMillan
Dan Werdowatz, Josephson Werdowatz & Associates

SUBJECT INDEX

Page number refers to the first page of paper

AUTHOR INDEX

Page number refers to the first page of paper